D1603150

Launching Leaders

An Empowering Journey for a New Generation

By Steven A. Hitz

Foreword by Brian J. Grim, Ph.D.

Book cover design by Fly, New Zealand
Interior design and illustrations by Mycore, USA
Editing by Charles Limley
Second Edition
Printed in the United States of America

ISBN-13: 978-0-9853613-8-9
ISBN-10: 0-9853613-8-7

LAUNCHING LEADERS ONLINE COURSE

Do you like the Launching Leaders book? Check out the online course! It's full of high-quality video and interactive exercises, and is mobile-friendly. Together the book and course provide a powerful combination to create your future.

Here's some of what you'll get with the course:

- A process for planning your life
- A method for developing your core values
- An approach for adopting mentors
- Action steps for "The Formula"
- An assessment on whether you're living a double life
- An exercise to identify positive habits
- A plan for becoming financially fit
- Ideas for giving back - now

The Launching Leaders course has been changing lives in many parts of the world. Discover how to combine proven principles with your faith in your everyday life.

Visit the Launching Leaders website and try the first class for free!

www.LLworldwide.org

PRAISE FOR *LAUNCHING LEADERS*

Launching Leaders makes a real impact with the practical principles it covers in the context of a rich faith-based environment, where readers can learn the blessings of adopting universal principles and practices to their lives, no matter their faith tradition. This book unites people of faith in meaningful application that would never happen otherwise.

Fr. Tim Byron SJ
Manchester Universities' Catholic Chaplaincy

Steve's passion for helping millennials find fulfillment is contagious and *Launching Leaders* provides essential principles and practical tools that can inspire millennials to do just that. I have no doubt that many of the core concepts in this book can help guide millennials from around the globe toward a successful future.

Chris Folmsbee
President, Burlap (thinkburlap.com / @thinkburlap)

In *Launching Leaders*, Steve Hitz successfully empowers his readers with tangible ways to live wisely. Steve goes beyond inspiring; he takes on the role of a life coach. As he tells the compelling true stories of men and women who have lived well, he challenges his audience to pursue change. The simple yet thought-provoking exercises and practices in this book will empower readers to reflect and take ownership of their lives and growth. *Launching Leaders* is accessible, hopeful, and warm in its tone. I recommend it to individuals striving to live lives of intentionality.

Jacintha Murphy
Denver Seminary
Millennial

No matter your cultural background, your belief structure, or even where you see yourself in the so-called pecking order around you, the principles so very carefully elaborated within these pages will, if seriously undertaken, change your life. Seemingly simple, this book is comprehensive in its scope. Incredibly detailed in its patterned assignments, it gives readers the opportunity to reach much greater heights than previously thought possible. Enjoy and let your journey begin!

Richard Ball
CEO, Anytime Fitness New Zealand

I have heard it said that "change is inevitable, but progress is optional." I have used this statement as a CEO and leadership/thought leader to motivate employees in large corporations. However, when I read *Launching Leaders: An Empowering Journey for a New Generation*, it occurred to me how this principle can be used in our personal lives. With a unique blend of leadership acumen and spiritual insight, Steve Hitz lays out a step-by-step approach for how we can *progress* in our personal lives—not just live out our days. I recommend this book to anyone who wants to seriously empower their personal progress.

Rulon F. Stacey, Ph.D., FACHE
Managing Director, Navigant Leadership Institute
Chair, Board of Overseers, Malcolm Baldrige National Quality Award

---

Launching Leaders is a game changer for the Millennial generation and generations to follow. Its simple and precise language will help any reader across all disciplines of life to understand the value of living life to the fullest. This book will change lives around the world. I entreat you to get a copy and read it.

Matthew Davis
Refugee Education Counselor, Ghana, Africa
Millennial

Launching Leaders is an inspirational and understandable guide to aligning your everyday life with your faith in order to discover and fulfill the divine purpose for which you are on this earth. The Formula to attain this transcendence is set forth in *Launching Leaders* as a set of simple steps that, when combined, create a profound way to engage with one's world. These steps can be applied at any stage of life, and throughout one's entire life.

Lisa Larsen
Attorney

Launching Leaders: An Empowering Journey for a New Generation shares principles that allow individuals to take control of their destiny. It teaches how to plan and create a future that is in line with your individualized values and goals. Following the principles shared in the book allows one to achieve success by leveraging the power of God's natural laws. While the Millennial generation is the target audience, the principles taught are universally applicable and resonate with people of all ages. Anyone who thoughtfully, sincerely, and consistently applies the formulas and principles contained in this book will find success in their lives and will feel the joy of knowing they are living in a manner that allows God to sanction and bless their efforts.

Kenneth B. Allen
Dentist

DEDICATION

When I finished writing this book in early April 2016, the scent of spring was in the air. Birds were singing, the winter earth was in the process of renewal, and we humans were awakening too with newness within. The blossoms were caressing the air with their fragrance, the evenings were growing longer with light, the trees were showing that twinge of soft, light green preparing to emerge in fullness.

I dedicate this book to the heart of my renewal, the spring of my days, the love of my life—my wife Ginger.

ACKNOWLEDGEMENTS

I am indebted to the many Launching Leaders "family" members, true friends, mentors, faith leaders, and all who have provided the deep well from which I have drawn my bucket; indeed, the ink well from which I have drawn my pen.

Speaking for the founders of Launching Leaders Worldwide, Inc., we acknowledge the full team of advisory members, donors, and their families who have contributed greatly to this body of work, especially the contributions of our founder, James Ritchie, along with our other founders, Terry Pitts and Laurence Day. To the pioneers of Launching Leaders from New Zealand to Africa, from Fiji to Mexico, and indeed across the globe, thank you for your amazing dedication to such a great cause.

We offer a special acknowledgement and thanks to the great work of Charles Limley, our wonderful editor who has crystallized this work, as well as Ginger Hitz, Michael Leonard, and Elisabeth Sbanotto who helped shape the content of this book and whose insights are priceless.

Launching Leaders is the curriculum companion to the courses provided by Launching Leaders Worldwide, Inc., and is a repository of relevant know-how that will help readers get from here to there. From wherever "here" is to wherever "there" is, we invite you to begin a journey of discovery that will empower you to create your future.

TABLE OF CONTENTS

FOREWORD

Steve Hitz is a master at laying the foundation for happiness and success. Foundations, however, aren't always all that sexy. They're the parts of a structure that go unnoticed, that is, until they crack or aren't strong enough to weather the proverbial storms of life. Civil engineers spend years learning how to construct a solid foundation for buildings, roads, bridges, etc. But how much time do we spend building a solid foundation for the basic pillars of our lives?

We might spend years in school developing certain parts of life's foundation - the skills and knowledge needed for a job, for example. But, do we devote the same energy to the other parts of the foundation that are equally important to a full and holistic life?

Steve's book, *Launching Leaders: An Empowering Journey for a New Generation*, gives you just such an opportunity.

Launching Leaders puts you in touch with universal, proven principles that are intuitive to all, but they are not always the topics we explore with the same vigor as we might pursue academics (or sports or celebrity news, for that matter).

Tools provided for young adults in *Launching Leaders* help people at the beginning of life's grand journey gain the know-how to examine their lives, where they are now, and where they want to be. It helps them apply their faith and beliefs to the other important foundations of life: family, love, and how to spend the most valuable commodity to its fullest — TIME!

Embracing the Lord in the journey is at the core of *Launching Leaders*. "Spiritual but not religious" may describe you (though I don't believe them to be mutually exclusive), and this book helps you go from where you are now to a future of where you can become much more than just someone passing the time until retirement. *Launching Leaders* helps people in their 20s and 30s chart their course.

I can't recommend it highly enough because the real beauty of these empowering ideas is something Steve imparts in a non-judgmental and authentic way. He - and his book - are the real deal. Enjoy!

Brian J. Grim, Ph.D.
President
Religious Freedom & Business Foundation

INTRODUCTION

"They will declare: Every journey has been taken.
You shall respond: I have not been to see myself.

They will insist: Everything has been spoken.
You will reply: I have not had my say.

They will tell you: Everything has been done.
You shall reply: My way is not complete.

You are warned: Any way is long, any way is hard.
Fear not, You are the gate—you, the gatekeeper.
And you shall go through and on."

—*"Instructions for Wayfarers," Robert Fulghum*[1]

In 2008 I joined a team of successful business owners, professionals, and experts, and together we created a business and leadership training program called Launching Leaders. The primary goal of this program was to teach up-and-coming entrepreneurs and anyone else trying to build a career in the business world how to infuse their professional efforts with holistic living and spirituality.

The pilot program of Launching Leaders, which was held in New Zealand, was hugely successful, and in just a few years the program had grown to reach students in Fiji, Ghana, Zimbabwe, Nigeria, Australia, Indonesia, Mexico, Poland, and the United States. To help us organize and communicate all the ideas being taught in Launching Leaders, several of the program's co-founders worked together to write a book called *The Ministry of Business: How Correct Principles Magnify Business Success*. This book, along with the curriculum of Launching Leaders, proved to be incredibly influential among entrepreneurs and professionals in their 20s and 30s, and was even used in business courses at a handful of universities.

It wasn't long, however, before many of those who'd read the book and who'd participated in the Launching Leaders program started telling us that they wanted more than just tools for creating meaningful professional lives. They wanted to learn how they could create an *entire lifestyle* grounded in the ideas, teachings, and principles they valued most as individuals. They found power in what Launching Leaders had to say about weaving together spirituality and business, and they were hungry for more.

The 20- and 30-somethings we'd met through Launching Leaders were making it abundantly clear that they wanted to learn how to use their faith to solve the everyday problems and challenges they were facing in the real world. They didn't want their faith or spirituality to be relegated exclusively to formal worship. Instead, they wanted to see their spirituality become an active and guiding component of their day-to-day lifestyles. Many were searching for answers to the questions and challenges most pressing to their unique life circumstances, and they wanted their spiritual beliefs to help them find those answers.

After hearing from so many of our Launching Leaders students, we knew we needed to expand the scope of the program to address these deeper-seated questions and concerns, and so we went back to the drawing board. We decided to create an entirely new curriculum that would move far beyond teaching people how to bring together their personal values and business. Our new goal was to come up with a set of concepts, ideas, and concrete skills that would empower Millennials to bring their everyday lives into full alignment with God in order to create the happy, successful, and meaningful futures they desire.

As a result of all these changes, we renamed the program Launching Leaders Worldwide and, perhaps most relevant to you, I headed up a project to write a new book that would communicate the program's newly expanded vision. That book is *Launching Leaders*, the book you're holding in your hands. This book is our attempt to answer the questions and concerns voiced by Millennials around the world. Some of the issues we hear Millennials raise most often include questions and concerns such as:

- "I feel like I'm doing OK, but I often feel like I could probably be doing a lot more with my life. I wonder if I'm really doing everything God wants me to be doing, and if I'm becoming everything God wants me to become."

- "I'm definitely ready for the next step in life, but I don't know what that step is. I feel like I'm kind of stuck in neutral and am unsure what to do next."

- "I've been taught to have faith in God, but I don't know how to apply that faith to my actual life."

- "I believe that God cares about me, but I feel like I don't really see His presence in my day-to-day life. Does He really care about the boring routines and concerns of my everyday life?"

- "After I leave a worship service, I often feel like I'm living a double life—like I'm one person while I'm worshipping and another person at work. I feel like I'm not living true to the person I really want to be, but I honestly don't know how to bridge that gap. Is it possible to be successful in my professional, social, and personal life while also being consistent in how I live my faith?"

- "I just feel so busy all the time, and it starts to feel like there isn't enough time to take care of all my responsibilities and still find time to be spiritual. How can I make spirituality a bigger part of my everyday routines?"

If you've ever felt any of these concerns, you're not alone. These are actually very important questions to ask yourself, and this book will help you find the answers you're looking for. Implementing the concepts and skills you will learn in this book will empower you to bring all aspects of your life into full alignment with your faith, allowing you to imbue your day-to-day activities with an authentic and vibrant sense of purpose and meaning.

Frame Your Life, Create Your Future

Before you read any further, I'd like you to do a quick experiment. Make each of your hands into an "L" shape and hold them out in front of you so that the thumb of one hand touches the index finger of the other. Your fingers should be in the shape of a rectangle. Now close one eye and look through the rectangular opening your hands have made. What do you see? How does the frame of these "double L's" change your perspective? What happens to what you see when you move that "finger-frame" and point it at something else? The concept I want to illustrate with this little exercise is that when you make this finger-frame you instantly change the way you see what's in front of you. And just as the double L's of your finger-frame allow you to define precisely what goes into your vision of the world and what does not, so too has God given you the ability to define the person you can become and the lifestyle you lead. The double L's create a frame through which you control what you focus on and what you don't; it puts you in full control of the world you see and highlights the importance of perspective.

Too often, the world tries to make you view yourself, your reality, and your potential from an unhealthy and severely limiting perspective. The world tries to tell you that you're not enough. It tries to hold you up to impossible standards of beauty, misguided definitions of success, and confused notions of right and wrong. To make matters worse, it can sometimes be extremely difficult to get away from these unhealthy perspectives, especially since they tend to follow us around on our laptops, cell phones, and mobile devices. While having limitless amounts of information a mouse click or screen tap away is an incredible, life-changing blessing, it can also introduce all sorts of distractions and unhealthy perspectives.

In his book *Essentialism: The Disciplined Pursuit of Less*, Greg McKeown describes some of the potential stumbling blocks introduced by our high tech, information-saturated world when he writes: "It is not just information overload, it is opinion overload."[2] The problem is not the amount of information available; it's the unmanageable volume of unproductive, distracting, problematic opinions swirling around our digital worlds. How do we sift through the infinite information, opinions, ideas, and ideologies we encounter every time we turn on a device or go online? How do we create harmony out of the cacophony of voices drowning out our everyday lives? How do we carve out space for our own voices in a raging ocean of noise? How do we maintain a healthy perspective on life? How do we look beyond all these opinions and focus our sights on the identities, lifestyles, and realities we most desire?

Rather than trying to avoid this digital ocean of opinions and information—which would be very nearly impossible and would also cause you to lose out on incredible opportunities to learn and connect with others—the key is to figure out how to sift out the bad stuff and focus on the good. This book, along with the courses taught through Launching Leaders Worldwide, will give you a foundation of ideas and practices that will enable you to engage with the world around you while always staying focused on what matters most.

ately, we want you to know *who you are* and *where you're taking your life* you can find the happiness you want while also being an influence for good. We want you to ignore the unproductive perspectives of the world and focus on bringing your perspective into alignment with God's.

But we also know how difficult that can be. The world's voices are all around us, and they can at times be almost deafeningly loud. The world's perspectives can exert tremendous pressure, and it can be a real test of faith to stay true to yourself and what you believe.

During the 2015 New Zealand National Young Adult Convention, at which Launching Leaders played a leading role, one of the nearly 1,000 Millennials in attendance performed a powerful piece of spoken-word poetry that perfectly describes the pressures created by the world's expectations and perspectives:

"I want that no thighs touching skinny,
That muffin top absence skinny,
That maybe if I lose ten pounds he'll notice me skinny,
I want that skinny-type pretty; that blond hair blue eyes type pretty.

But whenever I look in that traitorous mirror all I see are those thunder thighs,
that muffin top type of pretty,
and that ten pounds I would've, should've, could've lost last week but no…
I'll try again next week, or not…
The problems begin when she walks past.
We are dying just to be her
Because beauty is thin, and not what's within."

After summarizing the world's perspective on who it thinks we are and how it thinks we should see ourselves, she concluded her piece with a call to see things differently:

"You are enough—in fact, you are so much more than enough.
Because true beauty isn't found in the contours of your face,
Or the shape of your body,
It is found in the root of your identity."[3]

Like this poet, *Launching Leaders* doesn't ask you to compare yourself to others, nor is it interested in how well you stack up to the world's notions of wealth, success, and popularity. Rather, it invites you to see yourself from a divine perspective, to start loving yourself wherever you're at in life, and to pursue the path God has set out for you. Instead of looking to the world to gauge your worth, this book will help you discover the true roots of your identity, and to begin living the unique purposes for which you were made.

In the same way that the finger-frame you made a few minutes ago gave you a new and different vision of the world in front of you, I—and everyone else at Launching Leaders Worldwide—hope this book will give you a new vision that will empower you to create a full and purposeful life. We invite you to frame your future in a bold and positive light, and then to do whatever's necessary to make that vision a reality.

Built on the idea that life is a journey of your own creating, *Launching Leaders* will help you envision what you want out of life. It will teach you how to bring that vision into alignment with God's vision of you and your potential. With a clear picture of who you are, who you want to become, and where you want to go, you'll learn how to get from where you are right now to wherever it is you hope to one day arrive. And it will show you how to fill the details of your daily walk with joy, contentment, purpose, and meaning, because the journey truly is as valuable as the destination.

Taken as a whole, *Launching Leaders* works to share spiritual insights, conceptual frameworks, and real world know-how that will empower you to first envision and then achieve the life you most desire. In so doing, you will cultivate the skills, abilities, and knowledge that will help you carry out a purposeful and complete life filled with service and joy.

My colleagues and I make no apologies for the ideas outlined in this book or for the source of these ideas. We firmly believe that the concepts in this book are inspired principles of faith, and that whatever, whoever, or however you worship, God wants nothing more than to see you be happy as you become the fullness of what you've been made to be. I hope that as you read, you'll feel the presence of the divine. I hope this book will inspire you to become your best possible self.

With that said, it's time to turn the page and get started. It's time to create your future!

CHAPTER 01

Taking Control of Your Life

"True freedom is where an individual's thoughts and actions are in alignment with that which is true, correct, and of honor—no matter the personal price."

— Bryant H. McGill [4]

In August 2015, two longtime shareholders and I were suddenly and unexpectedly asked to leave the business I'd founded 22 years earlier with my wife Ginger. After building it from the ground up, she and I had sold the company in 2010 to a new group of owners, who had initially asked me to stay on board in a supervisory position. But after five years of that arrangement, they decided it was time to part ways and, without any advance notice, they told me I had to leave.

This was probably the most difficult thing I'd ever had to deal with in my entire decades-long career as an entrepreneur and businessperson. As I left the building that day, a flood of mixed emotions overcame me—it felt like I had suddenly been thrown out into Class VI whitewater rapids with only a raft and a paddle to get me through.

In the weeks that followed, I found myself having a real identity crisis. My position as a successful business owner had apparently become a more central part in how I perceived my identity than I had previously realized. I had grown somewhat dependent on the sense of control that running my own company had given me. I had become accustomed to the sensation of being wrapped in a bubble or cocoon of success. Losing my job made me realize just how deeply we humans like being wrapped in our personal security blankets, and when those blankets are ripped away, we can often end up feeling naked, vulnerable, and exposed. That's exactly how I was feeling.

Still reeling from the shock and pain of the entire ordeal, I called one of my lifelong mentors for advice. He shared wise words with me when he said, "Everyone should have the experience of an unexpected transition at least once in their lifetime." He explained to me that some of life's most valuable lessons—the ones that have significance beyond the immediate here and now—are learned during moments of trial, hardship, and unexpected challenge. These kinds of "opportunities," although they may not initially look like it, are ultimately what teach us to focus on those things that really matter most in our lives.

Along with my mentor, Ginger also shared wise words that really helped in the healing process. Although she hadn't worked at the company since we sold it in 2010, she had been a key player in the founding, growth, and expansion of the business since day one. She knew the ins and outs of the entire company, and was able to provide some particularly valuable insights.

One day she turned to me and said, "Steve, we didn't build a company, we built a family." She was right. The thing that caused the most pain wasn't the bottom line, it was being forced away from the wonderful people I'd grown to love and care so much about.

As Ginger continued helping me recover from the shock of it all, we spent a great deal of time praying with each other and with our family. They helped me put everything into proper perspective, and I tried to focus on what I could learn from this experience. Although it was hard, I did my best to transform this incredibly painful time into a chance to renew my faith in and commitment to God.

By shifting my perspective (remember the finger-frame exercise from the Introduction?), I soon found that I'd developed a new level of empathy. I felt a deepened sense of concern and compassion for anyone who's ever lost a job, and who subsequently finds themselves floating down the river of unemployment, unsure what might be waiting around the next bend. I was reminded of how important it is for all of us to be humble, to resist the temptation to place ourselves above others, and to keep our lives focused on the spiritual side of things. This entire experience was a powerful—although incredibly painful—reminder that no matter how much we think we're in control, everything can change in a single instant. The only constant in life is God. And that's exactly why it's so important for us to learn how to bring all aspects of our lives into full alignment with God.

In the end, I was able to work through this difficult episode by relying on the love and guidance of family members and great mentors, and by trying my best to live according to the Cycle of Spiritual Guidance.

The Cycle of Spiritual Guidance is a core piece of what Launching Leaders Worldwide teaches, and it spells out exactly what a person needs to do in order to bring their life into alignment with God. Focusing on the Cycle of Spiritual Guidance fundamentally changed how I felt about the experience of losing my job. So much so, in fact, that what I eventually came to discover in this unexpected "occupational change" is that God will move any one of us from our comfort zones toward an incredible land of promise—wherever it is that God desires us to be.

If you open yourself to the power of the divine, *God WILL move you*. And the Cycle of Spiritual Guidance is what makes it all possible.

The Cycle Of Spiritual Guidance

The experience I just described is a great example of why we should avoid building our foundations on external factors like careers, wealth, or popularity. While having a good job, earning a living, and making meaningful connections with others are all incredibly important components of a well-rounded lifestyle, these things should not become the *foundation* of who we are and how we seek our happiness.

One of the biggest dangers of allowing external factors like these to become the foundation of our lives is that very often these are things we don't have control over. I had no control over what the new business owners thought about me, or their decision to ask me to leave. Although we can't control the unexpected difficulties and events in our lives, we can control how we respond to them. We can look to God for direction, insight, and peace.

Ultimately, the entire experience of losing my job was a good reminder that the key to happiness is taking control of our lives by consciously aligning ourselves with God. No matter what's going on around us, we have complete and total control over what we choose to build our identities and our happiness on. When you align yourself with God, you choose to build a life foundation that will help you stay strong, happy, and grounded through the good times, the bad times, and everything in between.

As you learn about and implement each step in the Cycle of Spiritual Guidance, you will begin bringing all aspects of who you are and how you live into alignment with the Lord. This alignment will become the foundation for a life filled with purpose, joy, and peace—even during those moments when it seems like everything is working against you. This is the foundation that will empower you to achieve your full potential. This is how you take control of your life.

The Cycle of Spiritual Guidance

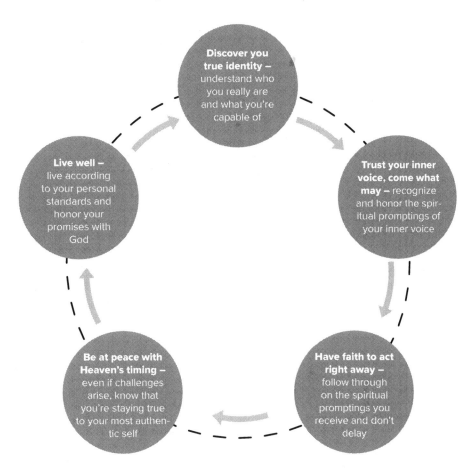

Discover your true identity: The first step in the Cycle of Spiritual Guidance is to recognize that you are an individual of worth. This knowledge needs to be at the very core of who you are and how you live. As you begin recognizing the spark of divinity within your soul, there will be no more reason to rely on external factors to determine your identity or your worth. This knowledge will give you a powerful sense of confidence that will imbue everything you do with meaning and joy.

In order for all of this to become powerful in your life you need to believe it and know it in the depths of your soul. And one of the best ways to develop this sense of your identity is to regularly set aside time to study, meditate, ponder, reflect, and pray—whatever you do to connect with the divine and tap into your spirituality. I suggest making this a sacred time when you separate yourself from family and friends, unplug from social media, and put work and school on momentary pause so you can have some quality alone time with God. Use these quiet moments for self-reflection. Focus on exploring the spirituality that resides at the core of your being and that connects you to the divine. This will help you know that you are indeed an individual of great worth with limitless potential.

As you make this the foundation of your sense of self, look to your faith community, mentors, teachers, and counselors to help you further discover and define your identity. As you continue cultivating your personal connection to the spiritual, you will eventually uncover the person you were meant to be.

When I lost my job I was reminded that careers, wealth, and outward success aren't what truly define our identities; it's our relationship with the divine. Instead of defining myself strictly in terms of my professional work or my financial status, I was reminded that my true identity resides in my existence as a spiritual being with limitless potential for happiness, purpose, and peace. Knowing this fills us with a sense of being connected to something and someone greater than ourselves, of having some purpose beyond just scraping through our own individual lives.

Trust your inner voice: In many ways, we are taught to distrust or ignore our emotions. We've been trained to assume that "acting out of emotion" is a fundamentally flawed or inferior way of making decisions. And while this is certainly true when our emotions compel us to engage in thoughtless, harmful, or dangerous behaviors, there are also many times when our emotions will actually lead us down wholesome and divinely appointed paths.

In fact, learning to understand our emotions is a critical part of bringing our lives into alignment with God's will. That's because emotions play a key role in the process of receiving and understanding the kind of inspiration that will guide us to success and happiness. In everyday language, we often talk about listening to our hearts. And you've probably heard people talk about the importance of following your inner voice. All of these terms and phrases are different ways of describing the same thing, the process of recognizing and understanding personal inspiration.

The Cycle of Spiritual Guidance is all about seeking out this kind of inspiration and then using it as the guiding principle for how we live and what we do. If you have a sudden thought or impression, or if you feel compelled to pursue one path or another, that could very well be your inner voice speaking to you, revealing a little spark of inspiration designed just for you. Sometimes you may experience feelings of comfort or warmth, and these emotions could be nudging you to do something. Other times, it may be a feeling of discomfort that's trying to tell you to avoid something.

Learning to discern inspiration is an important part of recognizing and developing your spiritual identity. Recognizing and honoring these moments of inspiration will bless your life with an underlying sense of peace and will help you move forward with faith, confident that you are pursuing a path toward purpose, peace, and authenticity.

Have faith to act right away: The more you learn to recognize your inner voice, the more important it will be for you to follow through on the moments of inspiration you receive. Responding to them right away, without delaying, is an act of faith that demonstrates that you are in the game, that you have decided that standing on the sidelines is no longer enough. When you act on inspiration, you demonstrate your gratitude for the spiritual aspects of your life and you put your faith to work in a real, tangible way. When you trust your inner voice enough to act on it, you prioritize spirituality, which ultimately helps you develop your spiritual identity even more. Simply put, when you follow through on the inspiration you receive, you open yourself up to even more divine guidance.

Whenever you're struck by a new bit of inspiration or whenever you feel like you've received spiritual guidance, write it down. Writing down your flashes of inspiration will help you recognize all the ways your heart speaks to you, and will make it easier to remember what you need to do in order to follow the guidance you receive throughout your lifetime. Acting right away does not mean you act thoughtlessly; it means you move forward with intention and with faith. When inspiration comes, believe that it will bless your life, and put your faith to work by acting on it immediately.

Be at peace with Heaven's timing: Learning to be at peace with Heaven's timing is perhaps the hardest step to follow. This is largely because we live in a *now* society—we've become so accustomed to immediate access and instant gratification that waiting for anything can sometimes feel frustrating.

But this is the step that really reminds us that we are striving to align ourselves with God, and that means that sometimes things won't happen as quickly as we'd like them to or in the manner we'd like them to. Being at peace with Heaven's timing pushes us to subsume our wishes and plans to the greater wisdom of God. It is an exercise in faith and humility.

There will be times in your life when you recognize a prompting from your inner voice, and even after acting on it immediately, you will still find yourself waiting for anything to come of your actions. When this happens it's easy to start feeling like your attempts to be faithful have gone unnoticed. But don't worry; God is aware of you.

In fact, when you find yourself in one of these situations, try changing your perspective so that you're focusing more on what you might be able to learn from that period of waiting. The space between acting on inspiration and seeing the final fruit of your actions is very often the space that determines your commitment to this entire process. At Launching Leaders Worldwide, we call this THE SPACE OF FAITH. These are the times when you will *grow into* the inspiration you've received.

Part of trying to live according to Heaven's timing is understanding that there are no coincidences. What might look to us like a random run-in with a new acquaintance or an inconsequential discovery of a book may in fact be a pivotal moment in the much larger timeframe of God. Maybe you reading this book at this precise moment in your life is one such "coincidence."

Another important thing to keep in mind is that sometimes you may have to continue doing something you felt inspired to do for an extended period of time before you begin seeing anything come of it. As an example, several years ago I had an impression that I should start writing in my journal. Believing that this impression was a flash of inspiration, and attempting to live the Cycle of Spiritual Guidance, I acted on the prompting right away. That very night I began writing. During the first few years, I had no clue why I'd felt so inspired to keep a journal. Eventually, though, when I found myself working with the Launching Leaders team and contemplating the prospects of writing a book, it became very clear what all those years of journal writing had been preparing me for. Not only had I preserved my past and found time to reflect more deeply on important events in my life, I had also sharpened my ability to communicate through writing. This became hugely important, as it allowed me to contribute to the Launching Leaders project in a meaningful way.

The main point in all this is that even if Heaven's timetable doesn't match up with yours, listening carefully to the promptings of your inner voice, having faith to act on those promptings right away, and trusting that things will somehow work out according to God's sometimes mysterious timetable are powerful tools that will bring your life, your identity, and your will into alignment with the divine.

Live well: Living well is the point at which you move your faith away from merely talking the talk and begin actually walking the walk. An important part of living the Cycle of Spiritual Guidance is trying your best to live a good and moral life. At Launching Leaders Worldwide we believe that staying true to your moral code is one of the most powerful ways to cultivate a holistic and authentic lifestyle. Such a lifestyle will, in turn, help you remain open to the promptings of your inner voice.

There have been numerous times when I've seen people receive a spiritual impression, act on it, and then, after losing patience when things didn't materialize as quickly as they thought they should have, end up slipping away from their moral grounding. They gave up while waiting, and they strayed from the moral principles that would have kept them closely aligned with God.

Living well will allow you to cultivate the discipline needed to move from the person you are today to the person you hope to become in the future. It will also bring you an abiding sense of peace, and will fill you with the positive, uplifting feelings that come from living a holistic life focused on goodness, service, and love.

Repeat: One of the amazing things about this entire cycle is that it never ends. It is ongoing through every day of our lives.

In fact, each step of the Cycle of Spiritual Guidance naturally feeds into the next. The more you cultivate your spiritual identity, the more tuned in you will be to your inner voice. As you do your best to act on the inspiration you receive, fully trusting in Heaven's timing and staying true to your moral code, the more you will see the spiritual side of your life blossom. This personal growth will confirm once again that you are an individual of worth, capable of greatness, at which point the entire cycle begins once again. As the saying goes: wash, rinse, repeat.

Final Thoughts

Incorporating the Cycle of Spiritual Guidance into your daily life is an act of faith that pushes you to actively believe and trust in your spiritual capabilities as well as your connection to a higher power. Because this cycle requires you to turn a vague and abstract faith into real and concrete action it is always a process of transformation. By living this cycle you embark on an incredible process of becoming. You will begin developing a powerful sense of confidence not based on worldly measures such as professional success or how much money you make. This type of confidence brings with it a peace that is hard to describe.

The Cycle of Spiritual Guidance transforms the way you see yourself and the way you approach your day-to-day life. This is why it's the first step in truly taking charge of your life. Now that you're familiar with the Cycle of Spiritual Guidance it's time to roll up your sleeves and begin the work of transformation.

Application and Relevance

1. Seek to understand your spiritual identity. This is the key to discovering your true worth, your full potential, and your connection to the divine.

2. Understand that the process of bringing your life into alignment with God will require WORK and will probably also require a change of direction. Trust that God will move you!

3. Temporarily detaching from electronics and social media can be a powerful way of giving yourself the space and time to cultivate your spiritual identity.

4. Learn to recognize the impressions of your heart by creating quiet time in which to pray, ponder, meditate, and pursue whichever practices help you connect with God or tap into your spirituality.

5. Act right away on the spiritual impressions of your heart, trusting that God has a plan, even if the timing of things doesn't seem to make sense.

6. Remember that living a good and moral life is the point at which we stop merely talking the talk of faith and begin walking the walk.

7. The Cycle of Spiritual Guidance:
   a. Discover your true identity
   b. Trust your inner voice
   c. Have faith to act right away
   d. Be at peace with Heaven's timing
   e. Live well
   f. Repeat throughout your life

Notes:

CHAPTER 02

Who Do You Want To Become? The Power of Defining Your Core Values

"Your beliefs become your thoughts, your thoughts become your words, your words become your actions, your actions become your habits, your habits become your values, your values become your destiny."

— Mahatma Gandhi[5]

In Chapter 1 you learned how to bring the foundations of your life into alignment with God by living the Cycle of Spiritual Guidance. Now it's time to figure out who you truly dream of becoming. When you have a clear sense of the type of person you hope to become, you can make concrete plans for getting from where you're at today to where you'd like to be in the future.

Ask yourself how you would describe the person you are right now. Now think about the ideal version of yourself, the person you'd most like to be in the future. How do these two people differ? What ideas and principles would you like to one day define you as a person? What will drive the way you make important life decisions? What about the way you choose to live your daily life? If you're totally honest with yourself there will always be a gap between where you're at right now and where you hope to be in the future. This isn't something you should feel bad about or that you should stress out about. In fact, that's actually the way it's supposed to be. Figuring out how to bridge that gap is a huge part of what life is all about. The answers to these questions play a key role in determining the kind of person you are today as well as who you will become tomorrow. To ensure that you put yourself on the path toward becoming your best possible self—the person God knows you can become—it's absolutely essential that you take time to clearly define your Core Values.

Core Values are a concrete set of beliefs, principles, and ideals that guide the way a person chooses to live their life, and that motivates them to become a better individual. Your Core Values will help you make difficult life decisions, and will also give you a clear set of criteria with which you can hold yourself accountable and gauge how well you're progressing toward your most important goals. This chapter will teach you how to identify and define your own highly personalized set of Core Values.

A Step-By-Step Guide For Establishing Your Core Values

Before you begin defining your Core Values, it's important to understand that this is a time intensive process. Figuring out the set of Core Values that will guide your life and define who you are is an important project, and it will require time and sincere effort. As you follow the steps outlined below, be sure to listen to the inspiration of your inner voice since, as we discussed in Chapter 1, this is a huge key to bringing your life into alignment with the divine.

Defining your Core Values is also a *dynamic* process. You should plan on returning to these values over and over again throughout your life, especially as you grow and develop. Doing so will ensure that you're always working toward a clearly defined goal of who you're striving to become.

Step 1: Find Holy Ground

Many faith traditions incorporate into their beliefs the idea of sacred space. In the Hebrew Bible, for example, the Lord told Moses: "Do not come any closer . . . Take off your sandals, for you are *standing on holy ground.*"[6] Similarly, Muslims remove their shoes before praying at mosque, Buddhists take their shoes off before entering stupas or other holy places, and we could extend this list even further. In each of these examples, removing one's shoes is a sign of respect and a way to prepare to enter into sacred space.

The main point of all this is that there is great spiritual power in establishing and entering into space that's been set aside as special and sacred. It's important for each of us to find our own personal "holy ground," a physical place where we can go to seek inspiration and spiritual guidance. This personal holy ground might be a church, the desert, the beach, your bedroom, sitting in your car at a favorite overlook, or any other place. Wherever it is, it needs to be a place where you feel comfortable thinking, pondering, meditating, or praying.

Step 2: Ponder

Once you've found your holy ground, use it to ponder the type of person you currently are. Next, think deeply and seriously about the type of person you want to become in the future—picture your ideal self. What sorts of things does that person do? How do they interact with others? What sorts of principles do they live by? What do you like about that person? In what ways is that person different from the person you are right now?

To reiterate, it's important to be honest with yourself during this step. Don't be afraid to confront your weaknesses or to look squarely at the things you might want to change about yourself. Learning to be honest with yourself, especially about the hard things, is a powerful tool that will enable you to grow and transform in incredible ways. If you're honest with yourself in this step, there will always be a gap between the person you are right now and the person you want to become in the future. And that's OK. In fact, recognizing this gap will help you identify what it is you truly value, what your deepest desires are, where your greatest hopes lie, and what you need to do to make them a reality.

Step 3: Write Core Value Statements

With the image of your ideal self firmly in mind, it's time to start making your abstract thoughts into something more concrete. You do this by writing Core Value Statements. Begin by writing down a specific key attribute of the ideal self you're envisioning. For example, one of the attributes I want to develop in my efforts to become my best possible self has to do with being an excellent communicator. Whatever attribute you've identified when you think about your ideal self, write it down. This is now a Core Value.

Now, define what this attribute means to you. I described what the attribute of being an effective communicator means to me this way: "Effective communication is listening intently, dialoging with respect, and being authentic."

Once you've done that, expand your definition into an active statement that articulates precisely how the attribute will become a part of your actual behaviors. Be as specific and concrete as possible.

Finally, end the statement with a positive affirmation, almost as if you'd already achieved the attribute you're writing about. This is an important step because it helps plant positive thoughts into your subconscious mind, and we really do become the things we spend the most time thinking about.

Combining all these steps, here's what my Core Value Statement for being an effective communicator looks like:

> "*Effective Communicator:* Effective communication is listening intently, dialoging with respect, and being authentic. [**Definition**] I will cultivate a style of communication that will inspire others. I will be transparent and authentic, while inviting healthy debate, respect, and mutual understanding. [**Active statement**] I am an effective communicator [**Positive affirmation**]."

Another example of one of my Core Values is striving to be a continuous learner. Here's what my statement for this value looks like:

> "*Continuous Learner:* I strive to be ever learning in both spiritual and

*secular studies. I believe in the 'daily bread' principle, which reminds me that I must feed myself with knowledge every single day. [**Definition**] I will fill my mind with teachings out of the great books. I will not waste my time in studies that do not add value to my life. [**Active statement**] I am a continuous learner and a pursuer of excellence. [**Positive affirmation**]"*

I've developed both of these Core Value Statements over the course of many years. As I grow, learn, and develop, I return to them over and over again to update and revise them. Sometimes I remove a phrase or sentence. Sometimes I change the language to more accurately reflect something I've learned. Sometimes I add new sentences that help clarify my vision.

The key is to write down statements like these for every attribute you see when you envision your ideal self. These attributes are now your Core Values, the things that will allow you to close the gap between where you're at today and where you want to be tomorrow. As with everything else in this process, take your time and don't rush it. Once you've written Core Value Statements for each of the attributes you identify in your ideal self, use them to gauge how well you're doing and to help you figure out what specific things you need to focus on in your quest to become your best possible self.

Step 4: Rank Your Core Values
As you start building your collection of Core Value Statements, take time to ponder each one. Try to rank them in order of importance. There may be some Core Values that don't fit well into any sort of ranking, but trying to establish some sort of ordered list can help you figure out where to focus your attention and efforts first so you don't feel overwhelmed trying to accomplish them all at once.

For example, if you put being an effective communicator at the top of your list of Core Values, then you know that's what you should focus on the most. This isn't to say that the other Core Values don't matter as much, or that you shouldn't try to develop them alongside the higher-ranking ones. This list is simply a tool to make the task of self-transformation a bit more concrete and actionable. It helps give you a solid starting place.

Step 5: Do Your Core Values Align With God?
As Chapter 1 pointed out, the key to life success is to align yourself with God.

This is especially true when it comes to developing your Core Values. After you've created a ranked list of all your Core Value Statements, return to your holy ground and ask yourself if what you've come up with aligns with your faith in the Lord. As you do this, pay attention to your inner voice to confirm that what you've done is good. The goal is to create a list of Core Values that the Heavens would smile upon.

Another powerful way to align your Core Values with God is to pair each of your Core Value Statements with a scriptural passage or spiritual statement that's meaningful to you. This will not only give you the confidence to know that you're building a life grounded in Godly principles, but will also help you see how your Core Values are reflected in scripture, how they're defined by scripture, and how they work in relation to other spiritual principles.

For example, a Jewish person with the Core Value of being open-minded could pair that value with a relevant passage from the Hebrew Bible or the Talmud. A Muslim might turn to the Quran for greater understanding of a Core Value, a Hindu might match a Core Value with a passage from The Bhagavad Gita, and so on. This practice will add new insight to the way you understand and define your Core Values, and can help inspire you in your attempts to make your Core Values a key part of your life.

Developing your own personalized set of Core Values that you know are in alignment with God is a powerful step in beginning the process of self-transformation. Return to your Core Value Statements throughout your life and let them guide how you make decisions, what you prioritize in your day-to-day life, and the type of person you're striving to become.

Application and Relevance

1. Remember that the whole point of defining your Core Values is to actually LIVE the values you describe. This is what will enable you to BECOME the person you would one day like to be.

2. Tap into the power of finding your own holy ground—this is your personal sacred space in which to pray, ponder, and meditate.

3. Use your Core Values to help you continually move forward in life. Even when you stumble, if you keep your sights fixed on progressing you will begin building a life of peace and purpose.

4. Understand that the process of becoming cannot be achieved alone; be sure your Core Values are in alignment with God.

5. Keep in mind that this is all part of a life-long process of TRANSFORMATION. Even though you won't yet be your best possible self, find joy in the process of change. This will help you LOVE the person you've already become as well as the person you're still in the process of becoming.

6. Follow the step-by-step guide for developing your Core Values:
   a. Find holy ground
   b. Ponder
   c. Write Core Value Statements
   d. Rank your Core Values
   e. Do your Core Values align with God?

Notes:

_____

_____

_____

_____

_____

_____

_____

_____

_____

_____

_____

_____

_____

_____

_____

_____

_____

_____

_____

_____

_____

_____

CHAPTER **03**

Mentors: Your Bridge to Success

"A mentor empowers a person to see a possible future, and believe it can be obtained."

— Shawn Hitchcock[7]

My wife, Ginger, and I participate in a sustainable farm with our daughter and son-in-law. The farm has everything from bees to cows, chickens to goats, veggies to fruit trees, and just about everything in between. I love this farm, and I'm particularly intrigued by the bees, which pollinate and bring life to so many of the other things growing on the land, especially the flowers and fruit trees.

The more I've learned about bees, the more intrigued I've become. It is estimated that a bee must visit two million flowers and fly somewhere around 55,000 miles to produce a single pound of honey. They accomplish this by cruising at about 15 miles per hour.[8] Researchers estimate that one bee can fly around the entire world on the energy it gets from just one ounce of honey—talk about efficiency! But by far one of the most interesting facts about bees is that although a single worker bee only produces about 1/12th a teaspoon of honey in its lifetime, an entire colony of bees produces anywhere from 60 to 100 pounds of honey per year.[9] This is the epitome of teamwork, and it highlights the old saying, "the whole is greater than the sum of its parts." The colony of bees working together as a team accomplishes significantly more than a thousand individual bees would flying around and working all by themselves.

This is also a perfect analogy for how humans function. Just as any individual bee can do so much more as part of a colony than it could ever do on its own, so too will we become much more productive with the help of others. By filling your life with good friends and mentors, your journey through life will never be lonely, and you will find yourself empowered to become more successful than you ever could all on your own. Along the way, you'll also become a friend and a mentor to others, enabling them to become better individuals as well.

The team of Launching Leaders Worldwide founders and directors feels so strongly about the importance of filling our lives with good people that we make it one of the program's top priorities to help connect participants with positive friends and powerful mentors. The way we see it, nobody succeeds alone. Everything we do exists within the context of large networks of friends, family members, teachers, church leaders, bosses, co-workers, customers, clients, and the list could go on and on. The main point in all this is that just as bees only succeed when they operate as a team, no individual person succeeds all on their own.

Because being part of a good team—a solid network of friends and mentors who will help lift you to higher ground—is such a crucial component of anyone's ability to achieve happiness and success, it's important that you take time to carefully and consciously consider who you're spending your time with. It's important that you seek out friends and mentors who will uplift, support, challenge, and inspire you. It's just as important that you strive to do the same for others.

Throughout this chapter, we're going to define "mentor" in a slightly more expanded way than most people usually do. Mentors are essentially life friends that we trust deeply, and who share guidance, insight, and wisdom that helps us bridge the gap between where we're at today and where we hope to be in the future. These life friends can be actual people we know and interact with, but they can also be great historical figures or positive and uplifting books— we consider any source of goodness and wisdom that helps us figure life out just a little bit better to be a mentor.

Seeking out and filling your life with good mentors is incredibly empowering. Life is hard, and going it alone can often feel like everything's an uphill battle. Sometimes it can feel like simply keeping up with the demands of daily life is about all we can handle, forget pursuing our life dreams. By the end of the day, the week, the month, the year it can easily feel like all we've done was barely keep from falling off the tracks. Meanwhile, our dreams slip away like a string of boxcars unhitched from the engine of life.

But when you find wise and supportive mentors, and as you begin sharing your dreams with them, you will feel a rush of relief. It will feel like a parachute has finally been opened and for the first time ever you can look around and enjoy the incredible view. Good mentors will share with you the insights, advice, expertise, and life lessons that will help you traverse the chasm that separates where you are today from where you want to be in the future. This is why *Launching Leaders* refers to mentors as your personal Bridge to Success.

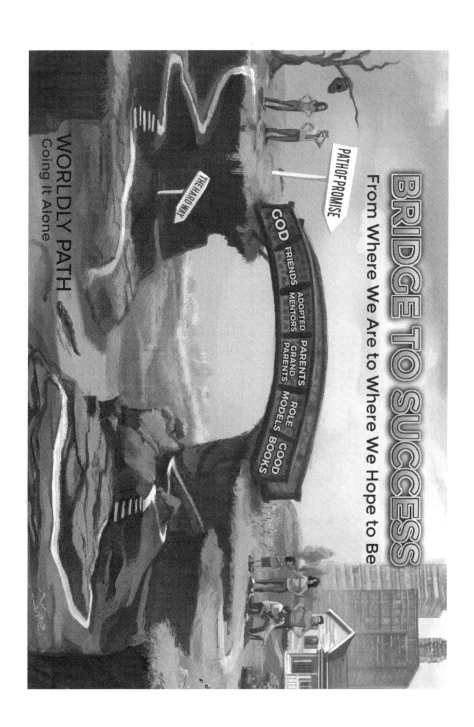

The Importance Of Keeping Good Company

I once came across an interesting quote that points out just how important it is for us to fill our lives with uplifting, positive, and inspiring people: "Do not company with fornicators—not because you are too good for them, but . . . because you are not good enough. Remember that bad situations can wear down even good people."[10] This quote is not teaching us to be self-righteous, judgmental, or to avoid serving or spending time with people who might be different from us. Rather, it's teaching us to be smart. It's reminding us of the need to have enough self-awareness to gauge our own strengths and weaknesses, to know when we can stick around, and when we need to run in order to maintain our own moral integrity.

Given the cacophony of voices, opinions, and pressures that constantly swirl around us, maintaining integrity to do what's right can already be difficult enough. Why hang around with people who make it even harder? When it comes to who you take advice from and who you spend the bulk of your time with, you need to pick people who share your general ethical outlook, people who will make it easier—not harder—to follow your moral compass. Again, this is not saying that you should be self-righteous or unfairly judgmental. It's a plea to be safe, smart, and to fill your life with the people who will inspire you and help you become your best possible self.

Perhaps a quote I like to use will summarize what I'm trying to get at here: "The good Lord said we had to love 'em, but we don't have to hang out with 'em." The people you fill your life with will become a huge part of the person you eventually become, so choose them wisely. Just as important as choosing the right kind of friends is choosing the right kind of mentors. The rest of the chapter will focus specifically on the power of having great mentors, and how you can find the mentors that are right for you.

The Role Of Good Mentors

To illustrate more concretely what good mentors actually contribute to a person's life, let me share a quick story from my own personal experience. I once had a friend who needed help coping with an addiction problem. I'd been encouraging him to seek out professional help, and in an effort to help him in that process, I researched rehab facilities and eventually made arrangements for him to be accepted into the one that would best meet his needs. I then physically got him there and walked him right up to the front door, but that was as far as I could take him. From there, it was up to him to actually walk through the doors and put in the hard work necessary to conquer the addictions that were tormenting him. Thankfully, he did just that and a few months later he emerged successful.

This story highlights a couple important things. First, it illustrates some of what was discussed above. In my efforts to keep good company, I offered what help I could to my friend, while at the same time making sure I kept myself safe and my moral code intact. I set clear boundaries in my relationship with this friend. These boundaries allowed me to maintain my personal moral code and empowered me to steer clear of my friend's harmful behaviors. They also helped us build an even stronger friendship with one another.

Second, this experience points out that as we strive to connect with others in positive and productive ways, we will find ourselves both being mentored and mentoring. My life has been blessed in invaluable ways by the loving help and support of some truly incredible mentors who I've come to rely on. In the story I just described, I happened to find myself serving in the role of mentor.

And finally, this anecdote highlights some key aspects of what mentors do. Good mentors help us see a way to move forward, they demonstrate hope and faith that we can accomplish our goals, and they give us the tools we need for success. But they can't do the hard work for us. It's up to us to use the help we receive from our mentors to do something productive.

How To Find Great Mentors

Good mentors don't just magically appear. You have to proactively seek them out. Below are the dos and don'ts of seeking out and finding the best possible mentors. As you follow these tips, use what you've learned in the previous chapters to remain open to the inspiration and promptings of your inner voice. Remember that the key to true happiness and success is to align all aspects of your life with God, and seeking mentors is no exception. As with any other important life endeavor, be sure to seek spiritual guidance in your quest to find good mentors.

- **"Frame" your future.** As you think about your future, consider your goals, your strengths, and especially your weaknesses. Think about the type of person you want to become and the specific skill sets you'll need in order to achieve your life goals and overcome your weaknesses. Look for mentors who can meet these specific needs.

- **Look for someone who believes in you.** The best mentors will believe in both you and God, and are actively striving to be a positive influence in the world.

- **Be observant.** Watch how successful people carry themselves, how they interact with others, and how they respond to challenges. Take note of who inspires you and who seems like they might have insights and experiences that could help you become the person you're trying to become.

- **Make it a spiritual pursuit.** Remember that Heaven's timing doesn't always match ours, and what might appear to be a coincidence could in fact be a divinely orchestrated event. Accept the idea that God cares about the details of your life and wants you to be successful and happy. When your inner voice confirms that a certain person is indeed the right one to become your mentor, take action and have faith that your "coincidental" meeting is a sign of mercy and love from God.

- **Be bold.** When you know you've found a possible mentor, ask that person outright if they would become your mentor. You may have to be bolder than you are in your usual interactions with people, but don't be afraid to be direct. As long as you're respectful and polite, most of the people you ask will probably appreciate your candidness. If you get nervous, ask yourself, "What's the worst thing that could happen?" You ask the person and they turn you down? If that happens, they probably wouldn't have been the right mentor anyway, so it's time to keep searching.

- **Be careful.** As you search for mentors, keep the following list of key attributes in mind:

  - Does this person believe in you? Effective mentors are great listeners and can always see the best in you. This doesn't mean they always agree with your insights, but you can trust them because you know they have your best interests at heart.

  - Great mentors are mentors for life. They take an interest in you as a person, and as you get to know each other better you will develop a meaningful friendship. Additionally, all great mentors *have* great mentors. Think about asking a potential mentor to tell you a bit about his or her own mentors and what they've learned from them.

- The relationship between a mentor and an apprentice should never be based on a financial arrangement. If a potential mentor wants to attach dollar signs to her or his relationship with you, it's probably not a good match.

- Great mentors will grow to care about you on a personal level. They will find sincere joy in your progress and success. In this way, great mentors are kind of like good parents, and their constant support will elevate you to entirely new levels of confidence and success.

Be A Good Person To Mentor

So far, we've been focusing primarily on what you should look for in a mentor, but remember that mentorship is a two-way street. Just as you should be looking for particular traits in a potential mentor, a good mentor will also be looking for particular traits in the person they choose to spend their time with. Their decision to mentor you will be based in part on their impressions of you and the reasons you are seeking them out. They will likely want to see some ambition and drive, along with a sense of humility and teachability. They will want to be sure that your values align with theirs.

Treat the process of finding a mentor kind of like a job interview, and focus on communicating openly and directly with the person you've asked to mentor you. Try to make a good first impression. Let them see your heart and know your intentions. Nothing goes further in these early interactions than sincerity and complete transparency. As leadership expert and scholar Vivek Wadhwa once wrote: "What you want in a mentor is someone who truly cares for you and who will look after your interests and not just their own. When you do come across the right person to mentor you, start by showing them that the time they spend with you is worthwhile."[11]

Another important part of recognizing the two-way road of mentorship is taking time to give back to your mentors. Be sure to not just take, but also to give. Look for opportunities to express gratitude to your mentors for everything they've given you and done for you.

Recently, I filmed a life long mentor as part of a training video we were making about the power of good mentorship. When the short film was finished, I mailed him a copy with a handwritten note expressing my gratitude for everything he's done for me over the years. A short time later, I used the video during a keynote address. The speech I gave was part of a conference for professionals working in the same industry this mentor had trained me in. Understanding that the audience would appreciate this mentor's expertise and contributions, I consciously used the video as a way to publicly honor him and to express how much he means to me. This type of two-way, give-and-take friendship is precisely the kind of love that is established through the process of great mentoring.

Final Thoughts: The Power Of Great Mentorship

Every successful person I've ever known or ever learned about had a number of great mentors. Pablo Picasso, for example, was heavily influenced by the Spanish painter Diego Velázquez, who was himself influenced by El Greco, who was influenced by Titian—you get the point.[12] It's a giant string of mentors and learners. In this pattern, one up-and-coming painter learned from an already established artist. Picasso mirrored Velázquez, ultimately taking what he learned and adapting it to create his own innovative artistic style.

Along with being mentored by the greats who went before him, Picasso also credited his father as one of the most important mentors of his life—sometimes we don't have to look very far to find a truly life-changing mentor.[13] After filling his life with great mentors, Picasso went on to become a truly prolific artist, producing an astonishing number of works. He completed right around 50,000 unique pieces, including approximately 2,000 paintings, 1,250 sculptures, and 12,000 drawings.

Like Picasso, your mentors will provide you with the inspiration, support, and wisdom you need to color the canvas of your own personal life. The goal is not to copy them, but to take what they share with you and customize it to the unique goals and circumstances of your life. Although the life you are painting is never complete—you're always growing, learning, and changing—great mentors will help expand the vision you have for your future. In short, effective mentors will help you navigate the potentially overwhelming world we live in. They will enable you to take whatever steps are necessary to create a truly brilliant future. They will help you turn the canvas of your life into a beautiful masterpiece. They will empower you.

Application and Relevance

1. No one succeeds alone. You MUST have many mentors to maximize your potential and live a joyful life.

2. Thoughtfully consider the types of mentors you need in order to meet your goals and aspirations. Great mentors will always uplift, inspire, and motivate.

3. As you work to find good mentors, seek spiritual guidance and inspiration. Rely on the Cycle of Spiritual Guidance and your Core Values to point you in the right direction.

4. Remember that mentorship is a two-way street. Become the type of person a mentor would love to work with. Be open and transparent with them, and make sure you and your mentors are aligned with one another in your faith in God.

5. Show gratitude for everything your mentors do for you. Mentorship is a life-long endeavor and should result in a continuously growing friendship and trust.

6. Become a great mentor and pay it forward; this is an important part of giving back.

Notes:

_____

_____

_____

_____

_____

_____

_____

_____

_____

_____

_____

_____

_____

_____

_____

_____

_____

_____

_____

_____

_____

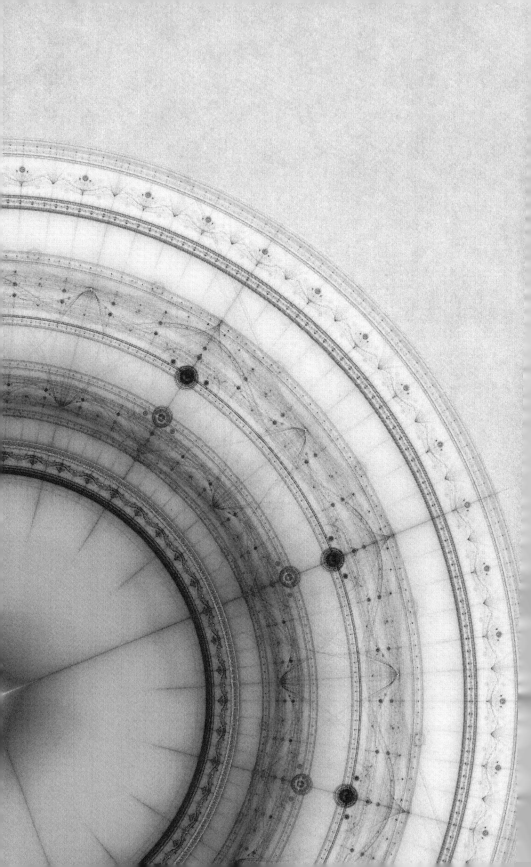

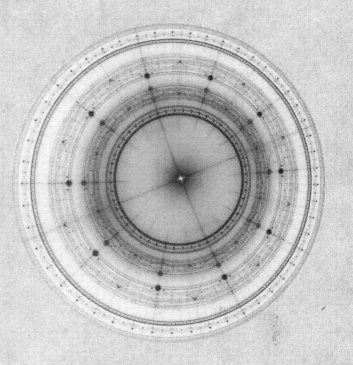

CHAPTER 04

Charting Your Course

"March on. Do not tarry. To go forward is to move toward perfection. March on, and fear not the thorns, or the sharp stones on life's path."

— Kahlil Gibran[14]

In the late 1980s, entirely out of the blue, I suddenly developed a fear of flying. Since my job at the time required me to travel to different parts of the country on a fairly regular basis, this strange new fear became a real dilemma.

My fear became so intense that Ginger once hatched a plan to try and get me onto a plane that was headed from Los Angeles to Kansas City. She borrowed a Valium pill from her mother, convinced me to swallow it about a half hour before my flight, and without me knowing it, had made arrangements for a flight attendant to personally escort me from the gate to my seat. Ginger carried out her plan perfectly. She dropped me off at the airport and started driving back home, assuming that I'd successfully boarded the plane.

Meanwhile, back at the airport, I'd become so terrified that despite Ginger's best efforts, I'd hopped into a taxicab and asked the driver to take me straight to our address. I actually beat Ginger back home. When she walked through the door, she was surprised to find me sitting there, feeling dejected and depressed. The only thing I was missing was a dark corner where I could curl up and cry. Needless to say, I felt horrible.

In facing this life obstacle, I believed God could help me, but I felt I hadn't exercised enough faith. So I met with some trusted spiritual advisors and we prayed together, asking God to give me strength to face my fears. I then decided to put my faith to a serious test by stepping out into the unknown: I signed up for flying lessons.

I will never forget how queasy I felt during that first lesson. My stomach was lodged in my throat, my hands were dripping with sweat, and my whole body was shaking like a leaf. By the time the first lesson came to a close, however, something miraculous had happened. As my teacher landed the plane, I felt a new sense of confidence bubbling up inside me, telling me that I could beat my fear. As we taxied toward the hangar, I was thrilled to have survived my first step into the unknown. The sense of confidence I felt reassured me that I was not alone.

Several lessons and eight full hours of flight time later, my instructor threw me back out into the unknown. As we were taxiing toward home base at the end of a lesson, he abruptly told me to stop the plane. He climbed out and said, "Go do three touch and go's, and I'll see you inside."

Alone in the cockpit for the first time ever, I thought to myself, "What on earth have I done?" My hands were shaking but I was determined to do what my teacher had told me to. As I prepared for takeoff, my training started to kick in. I sped down the runway and a few seconds later the wheels jumped off the asphalt. Just like that I was flying an airplane all by myself! As I made my circle around the airfield, I remembered that it wasn't too long ago that I was taking trains all the way to Kansas City because I was too paralyzed to fly. I didn't have time to daydream for too long, however, before I found myself facing yet another terrifying situation.

As I prepared for landing, I radioed in my position just as I'd been trained to: "Husky 334 Charlie Bravo, turning final runway 15." To my surprise—and to my sudden horror—I heard another voice come back over the radio: "United Express short final for 33." In airplane lingo, what this meant was that my first solo flight had somehow ended up on course for a head-on collision with a large commercial aircraft.

Maybe my radio wasn't working and no one had heard me, I frantically thought to myself. Maybe he didn't know I was there. I barked back with a shaky voice, "This is 334 Charlie Bravo. I'm on short final for 15 and this is my first solo flight, over." Then came the calm and somewhat amused voice of the other pilot: "United Express is breaking off final for 33. It's your runway buddy, and good luck. We'll go around."

That was the day I fell in love with aviation. I went on to fly across the country for many years after that. Flying allowed me to see the earth in an entirely different way, and it gave me a new perspective on all sorts of things. There are many other stories I could tell you from my years of flying. But for the purposes of this book, I want to use this specific story as a way to explore what it means to chart our course through life. The key to this entire experience is that I could not have overcome my fears or accomplished my goals alone. I needed the help and support of family members, loved ones, and spiritual advisors. I needed to seek God's help, and then put my faith to work by stepping out of my comfort zone. I needed mentors, training, and experience in the captain's seat before I was able to fly on my own. I needed a good deal of mercy and grace, just like when the commercial pilot had pity on a rookie flying his first solo mission.

In life, just as in learning to fly, charting your course toward success and happiness requires work. It requires that you do what's necessary to bring your life into alignment with God. It requires you to plan ahead, seek out mentors, study, and learn—you don't just jump into an airplane and expect to fly it. Charting a successful course through life means that you think about the goals that will help you become who and what you most desire, as well as the specific roles you'll need to fill to get there. Most importantly, charting a successful course means you're striving to follow God's vision for your life by listening to the inspiration of your inner voice.

Let's set out on this journey together. Now is the time to take your own leap of faith into the unknown, to overcome whatever fears or worries you may have, to break free from gravity, and to develop a life plan that will allow you to truly soar.

PHASE 1: Create Alignment; Envision Your Destination

Before you can begin plotting out any sort of course for your life, you've got to have a destination in mind—some objective for what you're trying to accomplish. And the best way to figure out precisely what type of person you should strive to become and what type of life you should work to achieve is to check in with God's vision for you. When you're focused on becoming who and what God wants you to become, you will be on the path to becoming your best possible self. Your efforts to align your life with God will bring a sense of peace and purpose that can't be found in any other way.

Fortunately, you've already learned how to align yourself with God. Living the Cycle of Spiritual Guidance, which was outlined in Chapter 1, and developing your Core Values, as taught in Chapter 2, is how you create alignment with God so that you can begin to discover the Lord's divine vision for you. The Cycle of Spiritual Guidance will help you tap into new levels of spirituality. Thoughtfully defining your Core Values will help you envision the person you're capable of becoming, and will give you a set of principles that will empower you to make that vision a reality.

Taken together, the Cycle of Spiritual Guidance and your Core Values are both about opening up your ability to access the power of your own spirituality. Think about them as ongoing processes throughout your life, not "one and done" projects. Living the Cycle of Spiritual Guidance and continually refining your Core Values is how you keep your life aligned with the divine, and how you create the strength you need to accomplish what might otherwise seem impossible.

Without spiritual guidance, and without a foundation of Core Values, it will be extremely difficult to plot a meaningful course toward life success. For this reason, if you have not yet taken the time to begin establishing your Core Values, you need to pause here and then resume reading once that's accomplished. You don't need to have every single Core Value fully pinned down, but the process of defining them needs to be well underway.

If you have begun living the Cycle of Spiritual Guidance, if you've taken the time to find your holy ground, and if you've pondered and meditated about the person you want to become, then you've already started figuring out some of your most important life goals. As long as you're working to maintain alignment with God, your inner voice will make clear to you what type of person and life you should be aiming for.

To stick with the aviation metaphor, these big picture visions and goals are the "destinations" you'll be flying toward. Now that you know where you're headed, it's time to figure out how to chart the course that will get you there.

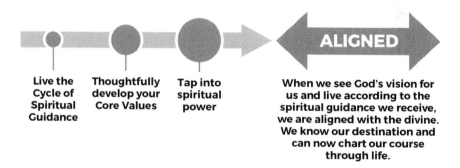

Live the Cycle of Spiritual Guidance

Thoughtfully develop your Core Values

Tap into spiritual power

ALIGNED

When we see God's vision for us and live according to the spiritual guidance we receive, we are aligned with the divine. We know our destination and can now chart our course through life.

PHASE 2: Chart Your Course

In aviation, we chart the course of a flight by mapping out a series of "waypoints," specific landmarks that help us get from the starting point to the destination. For example, a pilot starting in Denver and trying to get to New York City might begin by flying east for 500 miles until they arrive at the first waypoint. Once they've reached that waypoint, they adjust the path of the flight until they arrive at the next waypoint, and so on until they've finally arrived at their destination.

Waypoints are what help pilots stay on track. They break a long journey down into smaller, more doable sections. During the course of a flight, pilots often find themselves drifting slightly off route or having to adjust to unexpected obstacles and terrain. The intermediate landmarks provided by waypoints give pilots frequent chances to check in with their overall progress and to pull themselves back on track if they need to. Waypoints help pilots stay the course no matter what challenges might arise.

Just as pilots use waypoints to chart a course from their starting place to their destination, so too should we use personal waypoints to help us get from where we're at today to where we're trying to go.

Mapping out waypoints in your personal life will help keep you focused and moving in a positive direction. In *Essentialism: The Disciplined Pursuit of Less*, Greg McKeown suggests that we constantly ask ourselves, "Am I investing in the right activities?" This is an important question to consider since "there are far more activities and opportunities in the world than we have time and resources to invest in. And although many of them may be good, or even very good, the fact is that most are trivial and few are vital."[15] Creating markers, signposts, and waypoints in our lives is important because these are what will focus our life plans so we can fulfill all that God has in store for us. McKeown summarized it best when he wrote, "If you don't prioritize your life, someone else will."[16] Establishing waypoints is how you prioritize your life. It's how you give your life a fundamental sense of purpose and direction.

As we discussed above, your "destinations" are those big life goals that you've identified through the process of living the Cycle of Spiritual Guidance and thoughtfully developing your Core Values. These destinations are essentially long-term goals that define what you're trying to accomplish and who you're trying to become.

With those long-term goals in mind, you now need to chart out the specific waypoints that will keep you on track and enable you to eventually get to your destination. These waypoints are kind of like short-term goals. They are more immediate and simpler to accomplish than your long-term goals, but just like a pilot who links together all her waypoints until she arrives at her destination, accomplishing your short-term goals is what will propel you toward your ultimate objectives.

Before you start mapping out long-term and short-term goals—your destinations and your waypoints—there's one more thing you need to take into consideration. You need to think about the specific *roles* you must fill along the way. For example, when my flight instructor sent me out on my own to complete those first touch and go's, I moved from the role of "student" to that of "pilot in command." My changing roles carried with them different sets of priorities and responsibilities that altered the kinds of actions I needed to take. In the student role, my job was to observe and learn; in the pilot role, my job was to put into practice all the things I learned through those observations. Being aware of your different roles will help you make good, productive decisions. And whatever your role, remember that in aviation you're always safer with two pilots in the cockpit. Let God fill the role of co-pilot.

To bring everything together: living the Cycle of Spiritual Guidance and developing your Core Values is what creates alignment with God so that your long-term goals match a more divine vision of your life and potential. In order to achieve these long-term goals, you need to chart a series of smaller, more detailed goals that serve as waypoints. As you move from one short-term goal to another, be sure you remain aware of the different roles you need to fill. And throughout all of this, remember that the primary objective is to *transform* and *become* the person you're capable of becoming. This means that as you move from one waypoint to another, you need to consistently seek out spiritual guidance and live according to your Core Values.

Here's what the entire process of envisioning a destination and then charting a course toward that destination might look like for a person who wants to launch a career in conflict resolution:

Core Value		Destination
Be a peacemaker		Become a master in conflict resolution and establish a career as a marriage counselor

After seeking inspiration through living the Cycle of Spiritual Guidance, this person decided to make "be a peacemaker" a Core Value. They then felt prompted to make this Core Value the foundation of a possible career move, and decided to work toward becoming a marriage counselor. After going to their personal sacred place, praying and meditating to know if this goal would be aligned with God's will, and feeling God's approval in their hearts, they made it a long-term goal, one of their life destinations.

With this destination in mind, they then charted their course by mapping out a series of waypoints, complete with the roles they'd need to fill along the way:

Starting Place	Waypoint A	Waypoint B	Waypoint C	Waypoint D	Waypoint E	Destination
Where I am today	Finish bachelor's degree in Psychology	Enter graduate school within one year of finishing undergraduate degree	Begin internship in 2nd year of graduate school	Earn master's degree in Marriage & Family Therapy	Within 3 years of finishing master's degree, find a job or start own practice	Become master in conflict resolution and establish career as marriage counselor
Role: Person of faith	Role: Student	Role: Application writer	Role: Learner, Volunteer, Worker	Role: Student	Role: Employee, Entrepreneur	Role: Master in conflict resolution

Throughout this journey, some roles will always remain the same. For example, you should always be a person of faith seeking to maintain alignment with God. Other, more specific roles, however, will shift in and out of priority based on what you're focused on at the moment. The key is to always be conscious of your various roles and to maintain a focus on dynamic spirituality throughout your life.

As you chart your course, you can continue adding more detailed waypoints to help keep yourself focused and on track. These additional short-term goals may have to do with establishing timetables on which you'd like to achieve certain milestones, they may have to do with finances, or with figuring out ways to give back and serve others. Whatever waypoints you add need to be specific, concrete, measurable, and in line with God's vision for you. Your waypoints should help you progress toward whatever long-term life goals you're ultimately striving to achieve. The journeys you chart for yourself—complete with long-term destinations and short-term waypoints—need to be simple enough to visualize, concrete enough to monitor progress, and most importantly, aligned with God's vision for you.

PHASE 3: Fly the Course

A pilot can never actually fly the course that's been charted without a compass and a heading indicator that are both accurately calibrated in relation to true north. Compasses always rotate to indicate magnetic north and heading indicators are complex devices working on gyroscopes, vacuum pumps, magnets, and other specialized components. These devices help the pilot account for drift, the earth's rotation, and other variables.

While both of these tools are absolutely essential to a successful flight, they only work if the pilot regularly checks them. A good pilot will align the heading indicator every 10 or 15 minutes to be sure the plane stays on route. Likewise, good pilots know how to use a compass under any set of circumstances.

As we strive to fly the course we've charted for our lives, we need to be like a pilot, constantly checking in to know where we are in our progress, making adjustments, and doing our best to stay on course. But since life doesn't come with actual devices and pieces of equipment to keep us on track, we need to make God our constant reference point. We should look to the Lord as our personal true north as well as the compass and indicator helping us progress toward our full potential.

The Cycle of Spiritual Guidance and your Core Values are, once again, what will allow you to calibrate your life toward the true north of God. Without this reference point, you are lost. Frequent spiritual practice, following your inner voice, and staying true to your Core Values all play important parts in creating and maintaining your alignment with God. Using your personal holy ground as a sacred place where you can study sacred writings and spiritual insights, ponder, meditate, and connect with the divine is how you check in with your spiritual compass and your heavenly heading indicator. In order for your journey to succeed you need to remain humble and teachable enough to keep God by your side and to follow whatever inspiration you feel in your heart.

To make all this talk of compasses and heading indicators more concrete, here's a picture of an actual indicator in the middle of an actual flight:

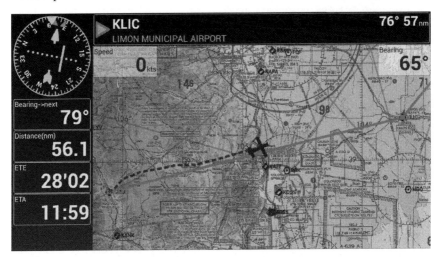

This map shows the charted course with a waypoint in the distance. Notice that at the moment this image was taken, the airplane is a little off course. And that's OK. In fact, it's fairly common for a pilot to arrive in the vicinity of a waypoint only to find she's drifted slightly off route. When this happens, don't panic. One of the reasons we use waypoints is to give ourselves regular checkpoints so that we always know how well we're progressing toward our destination. When you struggle getting to a waypoint, or you get there but realize you've drifted off course, use what you've learned in this book to check in with God and pull yourself back into alignment.

As you begin following the route you've charted, with God as your reference point, compass, and co-pilot, you'll see that the higher you fly, the more comprehensive your view becomes. There is safety in altitude, and as you continue charting your course and flying your waypoints, you will see more and more of God's vision for you.

Your Daily Walk

One final thing to consider in charting your course with God is your daily walk. We've talked a lot about destinations and waypoints, but what about the regular routines of your day-to-day life? How do you fly your charted course on a daily basis? One of the most powerful ways to implement the principles of this chapter into your daily life is to begin a daily devotional.

Your devotional should be a time that's set aside each day just for *you*. No distractions, just a quiet place—possibly your personal sacred place—to be alone with your thoughts and your heart. This is your time to fill your mind with uplifting ideas and to gain insights out of great books, including scripture. It's your time to meditate, pray, and make fine-tune adjustments to your heading indicator. Your devotional is your time to check in with yourself to be sure your daily walk is aligned with God, with the life path you've charted, and with your heart. This simple practice will produce incredible results, and will give you the fuel you need to continue your journey through life each day.

Along with everyone else at Launching Leaders Worldwide, I believe that establishing a plan for your life that's aligned with God and that helps map out what you're trying to accomplish in the long-term, the short-term, as well as on a daily basis increases your chances of creating a fruitful and abundant life. Doing so will give you a valuable sense of direction and purpose, and will help you know which path to take to avoid danger. Of course, even a clearly charted route flown by the best pilot in the world will still experience some degree of turbulence. But with a destination clearly in mind, your waypoints mapped out, and an active faith in God as your personal reference point, compass, and co-pilot, you will be well equipped to ride out the turbulence and continue on your way with confidence and joy. Charting your course with God will give you both guidance and protection. It will empower you to live a life of meaning and happiness now and into the future.

Application and Relevance

1. Now is the time to overcome your fears, take a leap of faith, and take the next step in life by charting your course with God.

2. Live the Cycle of Spiritual Guidance and thoughtfully develop your Core Values to create alignment with God.

3. Use your alignment with God to envision the long-term "destinations" you're working to achieve.

4. Develop short-term "waypoints" that will help keep you on track, and that will elevate your view so you can see God's vision for you. Reaching these short-term goals will give you an energizing sense of accomplishment to help you keep going.

5. Be sure your destinations and waypoints are simple, concrete, and measurable.

6. As you progress toward your waypoints, consider the different roles you'll need to adopt along the way. Always let God fill the role of co-pilot.

7. Begin a daily devotional to inspire your daily walk.

8. Start now and soar!

Notes:

_____

_____

_____

_____

_____

_____

_____

_____

_____

_____

_____

_____

_____

_____

_____

_____

_____

_____

_____

_____

_____

CHAPTER **05**

The Formula

"You were put on this earth to achieve your greatest self, to live out your purpose, and to do it courageously."

— Steve Maraboli[17]

One of my dear friends is a scientist who used to work for a dog food company that was owned by Nestlé. People usually associate that name with chocolate, but Nestlé actually owns a very diverse collection of companies, one of which makes pet food. In the late 1980s, my friend was working on developing the formula for a new line of "gourmet" dog food. He'd been working on the project for a long time and he'd just about figured it out. But there was still something lacking, and no matter how hard he thought about it, he just couldn't seem to get that final missing piece. He had no idea how to solve the mystery. He felt like he was banging his head against the wall trying to come up with some sort of solution, but nothing came.

Finally, at the height of his frustration, he decided that he needed to seek some sort of spiritual guidance to help get him through this obstacle. He went to his personal holy ground and spent time praying and meditating, looking for a solution. Eventually, he was inspired with some new ideas that helped him figure out the missing part of the formula.

The dog food he created came to be known as Grand Gourmet. My friend's formula quickly became one of the most iconic dog foods of all time, thanks largely to a famous TV commercial that showed a solid tubular chunk of "ordinary" dog food falling out of a can. This image was followed by footage of Grand Gourmet's signature "beefy strips, savory sauce" being poured out of a can. The narrator then asked, "If you were a dog, which one would you eat?" Not surprisingly, the dog in the commercial passes by the ordinary dog food and goes straight for the juicy morsels of Grand Gourmet.

My friend's dog food proved to be one of the most important innovations in the entire pet food industry. While Nestlé's competitors at the time were selling a can of dog food for around 50 cents, Grand Gourmet sold for 69 cents a can. This was the start of the gourmet dog food market, a sector that now tops several billion dollars in annual sales. The creation of Grand Gourmet is what launched my friend's career. After this initial success, he was put in charge of research and development for the company's entire pet food division. He was hugely successful in his field, and went on to complete an incredible career in style.

This story is literally about the discovery of a formula that led my friend down the path toward success. That makes it the perfect way to start this chapter, since this section of the book is also about a "formula" that, if applied, will change every aspect of your life. The Formula you will learn in this chapter will help you move way beyond the ordinary, much like my friend's dog food formula allowed him to become *extraordinary* in his professional career.

The Formula I'm talking about was created and developed by Jim Ritchie. Ginger and I met Jim in 1978, shortly after he'd retired from a wildly successful entrepreneurial career at the ripe age of 35. We quickly adopted him as our mentor, and over the course of the next few years, he introduced us to several powerful ideas—most of which have actually found their way into this book.

The combination of my curiosity and Jim's willingness to teach and share soon led to a special friendship that I often compare to the relationship between Mr. Miyagi and Daniel Larusso in the film *The Karate Kid*. Every Saturday morning, I would arrive at the Ritchie's home to chat with my self-adopted mentor, my personal Mr. Miyagi. As Jim sat in his Winnebago reading the newspaper, he would eventually pause what he was reading, look at me over the top of his paper, and give me tidbits of advice and instruction before sending me on my way. I'd then spend the rest of the week thinking about what he'd told me and working to incorporate his advice into my life. When Saturday rolled around again, I'd be back in Jim's Winnebago ready to learn more. This pattern continued for some time, until he finally entrusted me with "The Formula."

Now fast-forward twenty-plus years, after we'd all pursued our various paths through life. Ginger and I had gone on to successfully build our own company. Jim and his wife had headed up a number of volunteer organizations whose work spanned four continents. They were now leading an entrepreneurial business program at a major university in Hawaii, and they had asked Ginger and me to come and share our experiences with their students. Because The Formula had become the foundation of so much of the success Ginger and I had achieved, our presentation naturally revolved around many of its key ideas.

At the conclusion of our presentation, Jim sat thinking about the correct principles he'd both lived and taught over the years. He pondered the impact these principles had made on so many lives, and considered how many more lives would yet be touched. He leaned back in his chair, and with tears streaming down his cheeks, said, "It really works. The Formula really works."

Indeed, since that moment we have worked hard to live and teach The Formula, and to put it into the context of a larger plan for attaining life success. That larger plan is precisely what's taught in Launching Leaders Worldwide and in the pages of this book. When combined with all the other principles outlined in *Launching Leaders*, The Formula is the key to maximizing success and living a joyful, abundant life. The Formula was born out of inspiration, it's helped put many people—myself included—on the path to success, and it has proven to be the real deal. It has changed my and my family's world, and will no doubt change yours. Now, in his own words, Jim Ritchie will share with you . . .

The Formula

The Formula is NOT a get rich quick scheme. I don't believe in those and they are almost never based on correct principles. Rather, The Formula is something I've learned from various mentors and sources, and have applied to my own life. After experiencing firsthand the power of The Formula, I've spent the last four decades sharing it with thousands of people around the world. It has worked miracles for me, for others, and I promise it will do the same for you if you catch the spirit of its message.

The genesis of The Formula was on board a ferry crossing the River Clyde, just outside of Glasgow, Scotland. It was October 1964 and I had left my home in the United States almost two years earlier to serve as a volunteer minister for my church. At the time of the ferry ride, I was actually preparing to go back home. While aboard the ferry, I was talking about my plans for the future with a close spiritual mentor of mine, a man named David B. Haight. During our conversation, as we leaned against the rail of the ferry, he looked at me and with a sincere and lowered voice said, "When you return home, be sure to 1) get your education, 2) make your mark, and 3) get prepared to be of service."

A short time later, as I sat on the long flight back to the U.S., I played these simple instructions over and over again in my head. What he said seemed so simple, but I felt like there was something more to it than might first meet the eye. Was I trying to make too much of such ordinary advice? Was there a hidden key to what he'd said that I had somehow missed? Or maybe he'd given me a clue and it was now up to me to complete the treasure hunt? The more I thought about it, the more I began to see how the three pieces of his advice might work together to sketch out some sort of formula for how to approach life.

Upon my return home, and while in the process of getting my education, I read J. Paul Getty's classic book *How to Be Rich*. Getty made his mark in the oil business in the 1950s, and was ranked as one of the top 100 business people to ever live. Wealth didn't make the man, but having made his mark in a big way, the wealth he accumulated enabled him to give back in some wonderful ways. In his book, he outlined his own three-step process for success: 1) get up early, 2) work hard, and 3) find your oil.

I immediately saw parallels between Haight's advice and Getty's advice, and decided to see what would happen if I put them both together. Doing so gave me The Formula, a powerful six-step framework for living a joyful and abundant life.

J. Paul Getty +	David B. Haight =	THE FORMULA
1. Get Up Early	1. Get Your Education	1. Get Up Early
2. Work Hard	2. Make Your Mark	2. Work Hard
3. Find Oil	3. Give Back	3. Get Your Education
		4. Find Your Oil
		5. Mark Your Mark
		6. Give Back

1. Get Up Early

The philosopher Aristotle suggested some potential benefits to keeping an early schedule: "It is well to be up before day-break, for such a habit contributes to health, wealth, and wisdom."[18] Benjamin Franklin eventually built onto this to coin his own well-known maxim: "Early to bed and early to rise makes a man healthy, wealthy, and wise."[19]

Interestingly, research has actually provided some concrete truth to support these suggestions to get up early. Studies have shown that students who wake up early tend to have higher grade point averages than students who sleep away the morning hours.[20] But it's not the GPA advantage that most benefits the early riser. Rather, it's the quiet, reflective moments you have early in your day that will connect your mind and heart, Heaven and earth, in some extremely powerful ways.

The early morning hours are what I call the "magic hours," and if you use them well, they will allow you to get every day off to a positive, productive, and meaningful start. This is a great time to put into practice the ideas you learned in Chapter 4 by completing your daily devotional and working to chart your course with God. It's a great time to exercise, read, and pray, thereby invigorating your body, mind, and soul. All of this requires self-discipline, which is itself a crucial component of life success. The "magic hours" of the early morning are also a great time to simply take a moment to enjoy the serene beauty of the sunrise.

2. Work Hard

There's a lot of truth in the old saying, "there's no free lunch." Hard work has been a main tenet of every successful person I've ever known. There is a big difference, however, between working hard and just staying busy. As you apply the principles you learn in *Launching Leaders*, you will find the balance and focus you need to ensure that your hard work is productive and meaningful, rather than simply busy-work.

Words such as "tenacity," "perseverance," and "dedication" are, in my mind, synonymous with what it means to work hard. I love what world-famous author Stephen King has to say about hard work: "Talent is a dreadfully cheap commodity, cheaper than table salt. What separates the talented individual from the successful one is a lot of hard work and study; a constant process of honing."[21]

I also believe hard work is good for the soul. I believe that devoting our sincerest efforts toward progressing as individuals is essential to understanding God's vision for us and our potential. Hard work doesn't necessarily mean it's only physical in nature. It also includes the hard work of the mind and soul as we strive to align ourselves with God.

3. Get Your Education

In your pursuit of excellence, it's absolutely critical that you acquire the specific knowledge and skills you'll need to become your best possible self. In doing this, keep in mind that not all education is officially accredited—ALL forms of learning count.

However you go about doing it, the most important thing is to develop a thirst for knowledge and a passion for lifelong learning. Becoming educated and well trained might prepare you to enter the market more confidently, it might give you the practical know-how you need to perform a challenging task, it might provide you with insights that will help you nurture your children and others around you. Whatever you're passionate about, and whatever goals you're working toward, seek out the best minds in your field, learn what they do, and listen to what they have to share. This is what it means to be a lifelong learner. Becoming learned in many skills, both with your hands and your mind, is an adventure that makes life all the more meaningful.

Given the way that our current academic system focuses so much on learning that is strictly intellectual in nature, let me remind you that a key part of getting an education is also learning spiritually as well. Living the Cycle of Spiritual Guidance will help you learn invaluable truths and insights. Be sure that your attempts to become a lifelong learner include studying scripture and other sacred texts, meditating, pondering, and being tuned in to the inspiration of your inner voice.

4. Find Your Oil

When I first read Getty's stuff about "finding oil" I thought it was kind of funny—as if we can all just wander outside and strike oil! But when I stopped laughing and thought about it a bit more seriously, I began to see the wisdom in what Getty was saying. To be successful, we all have to discover that thing—that life pursuit—that truly excites, motivates, and empowers us. When we're actively pursuing our life passion, we'll naturally be propelled toward greatness, toward making some meaningful contribution that extends beyond just our own selves. This is what it means to "find your oil."

In his book, Getty is clear that money and riches are not the oil he's talking about. Rather, finding your oil has to do with finding something you love and are passionate about, and then using that enthusiasm to contribute something great and of worth. Finding your oil means that you live a life guided by what you value and find important rather than a life driven by the expectations of others. As Getty puts it:

> *"To be truly rich, regardless of his fortune or lack of it, a man must live by his own values. If those values are not personally meaningful, then no amount of money gained can hide the emptiness of a life without them.*

I have known entirely too many people who spend their lives doing what others expect of them to do. They force themselves into patterns of behavior which have been established for—and by—people with personalities entirely different from their own. Seeking to conform to those patterns, they dissolve into grotesque, blurred mirror images as they obliterate their individuality to imitate others. Rootless, dissatisfied, they strive frantically—and most often vainly—to find their own identities within the constricting limits of an existence alien to their natures, instincts, and innate desires.[22]

Finding your personal oil is about discovering your true identity, being your true self, and living out the righteous desires of your heart. And as you've already learned, the best way to make these discoveries is by grounding your daily walk in a meaningful connection with the spiritual side of your life.

When a person truly LOVES what they're involved in, the rewards take care of themselves. Too many people have lived their lives trapped in a rut that doesn't spark any joy for them, controlled by fear and resigned to "just getting along." Why let the world—filled with its cacophony of expectations, ideas, and opinions—dictate what your dreams should be or keep you from realizing those desires that truly matter to you? Being great at whatever it is you decide to do will become much easier if you also love what you do. Find your oil.

5. Make Your Mark

In simple terms, making your mark means making a difference. Throughout my years of mentoring and teaching, I always ask young people, "How will the world be different because you lived?" Indeed, we all can and should make a positive difference in the lives of those around us.

There are so many possible ways to make your mark and contribute something distinctive to the world that it'd be impossible to list them all. No matter what a person's job, wealth, career, or life circumstance, we can all find a way to make a positive mark on the world around us. Your mark could be an innovative development in your professional field, just like Steve's scientist friend did in the world of pet food. It could be an act of service that makes a positive change for your community. Whatever it is, strive to make the world a little bit better.

This step follows immediately after "Find Your Oil" for a reason. As you find that which you are passionate about, and as you become great at doing that thing, you will naturally begin positioning yourself to make your mark on the world in a positive way. As you strive to be a positive influence in the lives of those around you, you build such personal attributes as respect, integrity, self-worth, and confidence. These, in turn, open pathways to accomplishing the next and final step in The Formula: serving others and giving back.

6. Give Back

These two words make The Formula different from every other self-help catch phrase and all the other "formulas for success" I've ever come across. Each step in The Formula is designed to help you progress toward a successful, happy, and abundant life. But what makes The Formula so unique and so powerful is that your own happiness isn't the sole objective. Rather, the ultimate purpose of The Formula is to empower you to become a force for good in the world. You do this by preparing to serve others.

When you achieve a level of self-reliance and have lived an abundant life—financially, physically, and spiritually—you prepare yourself to give back in a number of different ways. And while having money can open up particular avenues for giving back, preparing to serve doesn't hinge solely on whether or not a person has monetary wealth. Instead, this step of The Formula is primarily focused on developing a loving heart.

Giving back and serving others generates the truest and happiest experiences of our lives. It is the most meaningful part of life's journey. As one of our Launching Leaders mentors in New Zealand likes to say: "Giving back adds the color to life." When we serve and give back, we should do so with humility and with a sincere effort to be as authentic and genuine as we can. Serving others is a way of highlighting the fact that nobody succeeds alone, and it's a way of entering into mutually beneficial relationships of love and care. Since we all rely on the Lord for our very being, when you serve others, you are trying to impart to somebody else what God has already done for you. When you serve, you recognize the sacred within yourself and within the person you're serving. Giving back is, therefore, another powerful way to bring your life into alignment with your deep spiritual identity.

Giving back can be manifest in various ways: giving time, donating money, mentoring somebody, taking the time to listen to a friend. The array of possible ways to serve is truly endless, and there are so many causes and needs that need our attention. But if we're constantly struggling just to keep our heads above water, it will be difficult to have the time, energy, or resources we need to truly dedicate ourselves to serving others. And that's where the power of The Formula comes in. Living The Formula puts you in the type of financial, physical, and spiritual position that will allow you to provide meaningful service in whatever ways you choose to give back.

To review, here's the entire Formula:

1. **Get Up Early:** Take advantage of the "magic hours," and use them to connect with Heaven.

2. **Work Hard:** Working hard will help you develop the attributes you need for success.

3. **Get Your Education:** Become a lifelong learner and remember that there are MANY other ways to learn besides the officially accredited ones.

4. **Find Your Oil:** Discover what you can become great at, what you're passionate about, and leverage that enthusiasm for the good of the world around you.

5. **Make Your Mark:** With humility, decide that the world will be a little better off because you lived.

6. **Give Back:** Giving back is what it's all about; express your gratitude for the life you have by giving back and helping those around you.

Hopefully you've started to see how the different parts of The Formula build on one another. We get up early to develop our minds, expand our hearts, and connect our daily lives with the divine and the sacred. We use that connection to help us work hard in body, mind, and spirit. We get all the education we can so that we can grow into our best possible selves. And as we tap into our full potential, we begin making our mark on the world in a positive, productive, and service-oriented manner.

To illustrate more concretely the way that The Formula has had a powerful impact on thousands of lives around the world, here's one quick example. In 2015, as we were preparing to do our first session of Launching Leaders in

Fiji, one of our instructors asked the principal of a local school if he could teach a handful of students The Formula. The principal agreed to let a group of students attend a class with our instructor for one hour a week. After the semester-long "experiment" was over, the students and principal provided notes on what they took away from the course. Here's what one student said:

> "I am now getting up at 4 a.m. for my solitude and planning time, then my studies and preparation for the day. I feel great about my days now when I get up early."

And here's what the principal had to say:

> "What are you feeding these kids—their marks have skyrocketed!"

The five students who took this experimental class went on to win all of the school's academic awards, and were instrumental in their school becoming the highest scoring in the nation on that year's standardized exams. After such amazing results, the class is still being taught, and students are lining up to take it. As Jim said that day in his university classroom, The Formula really works.

Application and Relevance

1. The six steps of The Formula are:
   a. Get Up Early
   b. Work Hard
   c. Get Your Education
   d. Find Your Oil
   e. Make Your Mark
   f. Give Back

2. The Formula will launch you into an amazing future.

3. Learning and living The Formula won't always be easy; it will require steady commitment, effort, and time. But the rewards are well worth it.

4. The most fulfilling aspect of life is serving others and giving back. The whole point of The Formula is to put you in a position where you can dedicate yourself to serving others and making the world a better place.

Notes:

CHAPTER 06

Beware the Double Life

"One of the great tragedies of life is that men seldom bridge the gulf between practice and profession, between doing and saying. A persistent schizophrenia leaves so many of us tragically divided against ourselves. On the one hand, we proudly profess certain sublime and noble principles, but on the other hand, we sadly practice the very antithesis of those principles. How often are our lives characterized by a high blood pressure of creeds and an anemia of deeds!"

— Martin Luther King, Jr. [23]

When we were developing the new Launching Leaders Worldwide curriculum, we had the chance to work with several groups of 20- and 30-somethings. One of the interesting things we noticed in our conversations with these Millennials was that some of them were adamant about the idea that our spiritual and professional lives should never intersect. They could perhaps be parallel aspects of a person's life, but they were still fundamentally different and distinct. Even among those Millennials who felt that faith plays a big role in helping a person establish a full and well-rounded lifestyle, some still said that the spiritual side of a person's life should be kept fully separate from the professional side of things.

This belief is part of a larger cultural idea that because we all lead complicated, multi-faceted lives, the best approach is to treat each individual facet of life as separate and distinct from all the others. The basic thought seems to be that since the different facets of our lives carry different expectations, responsibilities, and social interactions, we need to mold and change our behavior according to what we're doing, where we're at, and who we're with.

In some ways, this approach makes sense. For example, you probably don't act the exact same way at a place of worship and at work. When you attend church, synagogue, mosque, or wherever else you go to worship, you might find yourself praying openly and publicly. And in that context, such an act is not only appropriate, but is very likely helpful and productive. At work, though, it's probably most appropriate to say a silent prayer to yourself, or to find a more private place to pray. These kinds of adjustments are good, and will help you be a socially aware and sensitive person.

But what we were hearing was something more fundamental than making slight adjustments to our behavior in order to be socially appropriate. It seemed that many people have been convinced that the best way to approach life itself is to see it as a collection of separate threads that are so inherently different from one another that we should never let them intersect.

We suggest, however, that this might *not* be the best approach to life. When we try to break our lives down into multiple distinct segments, and then try to become a different person for each one, what we're really doing is introducing all sorts of gaps into who we are and how we're trying to live. Attempting to straddle these gaps by living with a foot on each side of the divide causes conflict and incongruence. It's a fundamentally inauthentic way of living.

Ultimately, breaking your life apart into separate and distinct segments makes it impossible to consistently live your moral code in all aspects of life, regardless of what you're doing, where you are, or who you're with. This segmented approach to life also fails to recognize that the same principles of respect, honor, kindness, professionalism, and courtesy do in fact apply across the board, whether it's our attempts to be a good businessperson, our attempts to be a good friend, or our attempts to be a good, ethical person in general. Rather than trying to break our lives apart into multiple segments, we should try to live authentically by pursuing a more unified, consistent, and holistic life. Doing so will put us on the path toward true happiness and success.

The Power Of Congruency

When a person insists on breaking life up into multiple distinct segments, and then becomes a different person in each of these segments, what they're really doing is living a double life. In the movies, having a double life is usually associated with the world of spies or double agents. And as anyone who's ever seen a spy movie knows, a double life can only be maintained through a complicated web of secrets, lies, and deceit.

Although spy movies are mostly just fun pieces of fiction, far too many people are living dangerous double lives in the real world. In fact, researchers have identified some disturbing trends that highlight just how widespread this problem is becoming. One study found that 70 percent of all men and 50 percent of all women will cheat on their spouse at some point in their life.[24] Similarly, a 2012 survey discovered that nearly half of all married couples hide expenses from each other or horde cash from one another.[25] Shockingly, some experts speculate that Millennial couples are twice as likely as senior couples to commit these types of financial infidelity.[26] All of this implies that the vast majority of all people will live an overtly deceitful double life at some point.

But living a double life isn't limited to just the realm of marriage and relationships; nor is it limited to only those huge, completely obvious acts of cheating, lying, and deceiving. A person leads a double life any time they compromise their morals or fail to live with full integrity. The double life could be a big and blatant act of lying or cheating, but it might also be a seemingly small or harmless deception as well. Maybe we're not as fully honest as we should be in our interactions with others, or maybe we're presenting ourselves to others in a way that isn't entirely accurate or authentic. These small, everyday deceptions are harder to detect than cheating on a spouse, but they are still moments of incongruent and duplicitous living.

With that said, it's important to remember that having moments of dishonesty or momentary slip-ups is a natural part of being human. None of us are perfect, after all. The key, however, is to not just give in to these imperfections, but to recognize them and then do our best to become a little bit better each and every day. Recognizing the imperfections of our human nature also highlights the fact that we will *all* live a double life at one time or another. And that's precisely why it's so important for all of us to learn how to avoid the tendency to live a duplicitous life—even in the smallest, most innocent-looking acts of dishonesty. This is a key part of the journey for each one of us.

One of the reasons it's so important to focus on avoiding duplicitous living is because even simple acts of dishonesty are harmful in a number of different ways. Psychologists have said that trying to juggle different standards and lifestyles—being one person in one setting and another person in a different setting—can create significant stress and harm to the person doing the juggling. It can introduce feelings of shame and guilt. And very often, what starts out as a small, seemingly harmless deception can grow into something much larger. The longer a person tries to maintain a segmented life, the deeper they get pulled in, and they eventually end up developing two or more different selves who act in increasingly different ways. Some of these selves can end up doing things that are markedly different from that person's "apparent" lifestyle. This juggling act is extremely difficult and stressful to maintain, and sooner or later, lying takes over that person's entire life.[27] But this kind of double life doesn't only harm the person trying to live it; it also hurts all the people they lie to and deceive along the way. Duplicitous living creates an ever-widening path of harm that affects a huge number of people.

At Launching Leaders Worldwide, we're concerned by the growing prevalence of duplicitous living because the more that people think it's OK to live this way, the more people will be harmed. The way we see it, the trend of cheating and lying identified by researchers grows directly out of the innocent-looking cultural belief that life should be approached as a series of unrelated threads or segments. It also stems from the closely related idea that our personal lives aren't anyone else's business so we should be able to live however we want to when we're away from church or work or family or whatever else.

The antidote to all of this—the seemingly benign idea that life should be segmented, the small, innocent-looking acts of dishonesty, as well as the more blatant examples of cheating, lying, and deceiving—is what we call the "congruent life." Living a congruent life means that you're focused on establishing *one* identity, *one* lifestyle, and *one* set of values that apply to *all* dimensions of your daily walk. Living a congruent life will bring harmony, peace, and a deep sense of well-being. It will empower you to forge through adversity without leaving your values behind. It is a truly authentic and holistic life.

Choosing to live a life that's built on the same set of standards no matter where you are, what you're doing, or who you're with is an absolutely essential component of taking control of your life. In Chapter 2, you spent time figuring out the type of person you want to become and then establishing the Core Values that will allow you to accomplish that goal. Remember that Core Values aren't only about your behavior. They're also about building character, establishing your motives in life, and creating a foundation of values and ideals. If you're not staying true to your Core Values in *all* aspects of your life, then what purpose are they really serving? The congruent life will help you get the most out of your Core Values, and in so doing, will help propel you toward your greatest life goals.

The kind of segmented life the world thinks is OK is simply not sustainable in the long run. Truly, there can be no duplicitous living if we desire the type of divine guidance and blessings we seek. When you stay true to your Core Values, which are fundamentally grounded in your pursuit of a spiritually informed life, you make it your top priority to honor and cultivate the divine purpose of your being—no matter what happens along the way. The spiritual truths to which you cling should apply equally to all settings and contexts. These truths are not temporary or momentary; they cannot be separated or compartmentalized according to circumstance.

Once you decide to live a life of congruency, a deep sense of trust, respect, peace, integrity, and abundance will follow. The great American writer Mark Twain once said, "The best thing about telling the truth is you never have to think about what to say."[28] The same can be said of living a life that is free of divided standards. When you remain consistent in your standards and values across all aspects of life, no one will ever question where you stand.

Keep Your Hand On The Tiller

Years ago I became infatuated with sailing. I think it was a natural outgrowth of my passion for flying; after all, sailing a boat and flying an airplane rely on many of the same principles. The more experienced I became at sailing, the more I fell in love with every aspect of it. I loved the ocean breeze and the spray that left salt on my lips. I loved the motion of the boat, and I loved the serene sense of being a tiny speck in the middle of a vast sea while also feeling at one with nature.

I started my sailing experience with an 18-foot sailing vessel. Some of the most important components on my first sailboat were the mainsheet, a rope that lets sailors control the speed of the boat, and the jib, a triangular shaped sail. The other key component was the tiller, which is a long curved handle attached to the rudder. The tiller is primarily responsible for controlling the direction of the boat. When you push the tiller to one side or the other, the rudder steers the boat in that direction. The boat moves especially well when the sails and tiller are all in harmony with one another.

While sailing, the boat's movement is very sensitive to the activity of the tiller; you can literally feel this sensitivity in your hands. To maintain control of the sailboat, you have to keep your hand on the tiller at all times. If I were sailing alone, I'd sit at the back of the boat with the mainsail and jib ropes within easy reach and my hand on the tiller. If I ever had to leave my post to unfurl a sail or to take care of something else not within my immediate reach, I'd use a rope to tie it in place. This would allow the boat to keep moving in the right direction for the minute or so that it would be unattended, but as soon as I'd completed whatever task had pulled me away, I immediately returned to my seat at the tiller.

When the sails were properly adjusted and the tiller was steady in my hand, everything clicked into place and the harmony of it all was amazing. In those moments, I was moving swiftly in the direction of my charted course. As I pulled in the mainsail for added speed the boat would heel over just a little bit and I could touch the bubbling water beneath me. I had total control over my speed and the axis of the boat in the water, and I could make precise adjustments to the boat's movement, all from my post in the rear of the boat. What a thrill it was to master these skills, and to be in full control.

If I were to suddenly let go of the tiller, however, everything would quickly fall apart. The boat would turn directly into the wind, the sails would flutter, and the boat would be dead in the water—or worse. Letting go of the tiller and the mainsheet for a brief moment was OK, but it wouldn't take very long at all for my progress and direction to come to a sudden halt.

In life, as in sailing, it's essential to always keep your hand on the tiller to ensure that you're moving in the right direction. When you fail to keep all aspects of your life in harmony with the values and principles that are most important to you, you're taking your hand off the tiller that guides your life. When you fail to consistently live your values and principles, you're leaving your fate to the winds. In contrast to this directionless floating, living a congruent life will enable you to keep your hand on the tiller at all times so that you're steadily progressing toward your most important life goals.

It's important to understand that when you take your hand off the tiller, you haven't accidentally *lost* control; you've deliberately *relinquished* control. Keeping your hand on the tiller requires conscientious effort. It takes hard work to consistently be the same person at all times and in all places, especially when no one is watching. Letting go can seem so easy, but once you give up control of the tiller, you've left yourself at the mercy of the wind and the waves. As you strive to keep your life in alignment with your Core Values and with the Lord, you will experience a sense of purpose and meaning that will empower you to steer your life toward true success.

There is nothing in this world like the feeling of being in full control of a sailboat. The power of the wind and the resistance of the water are truly breathtaking. But the only way to experience all this is to learn and utilize the skills that will keep the boat safely on its charted course. Distractions and diversions constantly arise, but a good helmsman will stay true to her purpose. If you want to accomplish your life goals, you need to be like the helmsman who tenaciously keeps her hand on the tiller at all times. Consistently living the values and principles that will help you progress toward your chosen destination will allow you to feel the power and joy of moving your life in a purposeful direction.

How Congruent Is Your Life?

Even when you're doing your best to keep your hand on the tiller, you will still experience challenges and trials. This is just how life works. The best sailor still runs into choppy waters and the calmest flight can still hit unexpected turbulence.

I remember once being a passenger on a flight where this is exactly what happened. While smoothly flying over the ocean, I was suddenly awakened by the captain's voice: "This is your captain speaking. Air traffic control has advised us of severe turbulence ahead." From my pilot training I knew that "severe turbulence" typically means "momentary loss of control," something no pilot—and certainly no passenger—ever wants to experience.

At that moment, I did a rapid-fire assessment of my life. If the 777 I was sitting in was suddenly swatted out of the sky, was I ready to face God? Had I accomplished my most important life goals? How close was I to becoming all that I'd wanted to become? What memories would I leave behind? Were there any secrets in my life that would tarnish my reputation or cause harm to my loved ones?

Everyone on board was relieved when, thirty minutes later, the pilot turned off the seat belt light. We'd made it through the turbulence, and the pilot's reassurances brought peace back to the minds of all the passengers. This was an important experience, though, as it gave me reason to pause and check in with myself. Asking myself all those questions pointed out some of the corrections I needed to make in my life, and also gave me some added motivation to make the necessary changes.

Asking ourselves difficult questions like this is an important part of tracking our progress. The only way to answer these types of questions in a positive way is if we're trying our best to live a congruent life. Of course, we all slip up, so be patient with yourself when you identify weaknesses that need improving. The most important thing is that you're consciously working to avoid the double life, and are striving instead to live a life of consistency, integrity, and congruence.

Achieving a life of harmony and congruence is challenging. As you check in with your progress, here are some things to look out for.

Signs that you're living a double life:	Signs that you're living a congruent life:
• **Secrets**. If the way you're living forces you to keep secrets you're probably living a double life. Secrets lead to lies, which lead to even more lies. Avoid this pitfall by living a congruent life. • **Gray is acceptable.** Telling half-truths, politicking to gain power, and spending too much of your life in the "gray area" between right and wrong is a sign that you're living a double life. • **Inappropriate relationships.** Any relationship that makes you question whether or not your behavior is appropriate is probably pulling you into a double life. • **Infidelity.** Remember that infidelity can take a number of forms: physical, emotional, and financial. • **Rationalizations.** Rationalizing away inappropriate, dishonest, or immoral actions is a hallmark of the double life. • **Misrepresenting yourself.** It's perfectly natural to try and present yourself in the best possible light. But if you carry this into the realm of telling partial truths or flat-out lying, you're on the path to a double life.	• **What you see is what you get.** Be yourself. Always strive to be your best possible self, but always be real. When everyone knows where you stand, you're living a congruent life. Your life will be especially rewarding if you consistently stand for great values. • **Integrity.** If you live your values with integrity, especially in the face of adversity, you are on the road toward the congruent life. • **Stand firm.** A hallmark of the congruent life is the ability to stand firm in what you believe, even if you find yourself and your values in the minority. • **Know when to seek help.** The key to getting yourself out of a double life is knowing when you're in trouble. In some cases, you may need professional help to overcome a particularly harmful lifestyle or to grapple with a secret addiction. Knowing when to seek help is a powerful sign that you're moving toward the congruent life.

Build Fortifications

So what do you do if you discover that you are living a double life? To begin with, this discovery is no reason to panic. Remember that being incongruent and inconsistent is a natural part of life. What's important is that you have the desire to overcome that inconsistency so you can live a more authentic, holistic, and spiritually informed life.

If you find yourself struggling with something that's pulling you into a double life—some sort of behavior not in line with the values you want to live or the person you want to become—you need to focus on putting up protective fences or fortifications to help keep you safe from whatever it is that's pulling you into that trap. Battles are not won without fortifications.

The first step to building fortifications is to identify problem areas in your life. If you find yourself engaging in high-risk behaviors that drag you down into a double life—behaviors like affairs, gambling, viewing pornography, or other secret addictions—then you need to address them immediately. You need to build fortifications, and sometimes that involves seeking help from others: a loved one, a religious leader, a psychologist, or some other professional. And of course, you should always turn to the Cycle of Spiritual Guidance to access the spiritual aid and power that will help you overcome weaknesses and pursue a more authentic life. The key is to check in with yourself, identify potential problems or weaknesses, and have the courage to seek help when you need it.

Finally, if you're stuck in a double life, do not give up hope. Psychologists point out that although a person's secret behavior may *seem* beyond their control, it's really a self-determined action that *can* be changed.[29] Even if the behavior requires professional help and outside support, it is always in your power to make positive life changes.

Congruency Is Always The Best Bet

I have a friend who is a great example of what it means to live a congruent life. He's a successful businessman who was at one point on the board of directors for a company he worked with. He's also a man of faith whose religious principles have taught him to value honesty and integrity.

At one point, the board on which my friend sat tried to cheat a man out of money their company owed him. Because my friend had decided during his young adult years that he would never live in the gray area when it comes to integrity, and because he believed in living a congruent life no matter what he was doing, where he was at, or who he was with, he stepped in and paid the debt the rest of the board had refused to honor. It would have been easy for my friend to go along with the board's decision by rationalizing that it was a business decision that required a different set of priorities and principles than the ones he lived by in his personal life. Instead, he stuck to his values. He chose to live the congruent life.

Ironically, my friend later had the chance to do business directly with the man whose contract he'd paid years earlier. Because of my friend's decision to act with honesty and integrity in their previous interaction, he ended up landing a new deal with this man worth ten times the amount of the original debt. Sometimes life works this way, but even if his decision to act with integrity and congruency hadn't paid off like this, he still slept well at night knowing that his values and morals remained intact.

Sometimes, living a congruent life may actually require you to pursue a more difficult, less profitable route. Jon M. Huntsman, chairman and founder of the Huntsman Corporation, which pulls in annual revenues of over $12 billion, tells such a story in his incredible book *Winners Never Cheat*. Mr. Huntsman had negotiated a deal in which the Huntsman Corporation agreed to sell a 40% share of one of their divisions to a chemical company for the price of $54 million. He and the CEO of the chemical company shook hands to seal the deal. It ended up taking the attorneys six months to iron out all the legalities, and during that time, changes in the price of raw materials dropped so dramatically that the division being sold was suddenly enjoying record profits. The value of the 40% share Huntsman had agreed to sell was now worth $250 million, nearly $200 million more than the price he and the CEO had agreed on.

In light of the division's new worth, the CEO of the acquiring company thought it would be unfair to not offer Huntsman a higher price. But Huntsman turned down the offer, saying, "I shook hands and made a deal for $54 million."[30] And that's the exact amount Huntsman's attorneys put down in the final draft of the agreement. After the sale was over, Huntsman said: "I could have forced them to pay an extra $200 million for that 40% ownership stake in my company. I never had to wrestle with my conscience or look over my shoulder. My word was my bond."[31]

The CEO of the chemical company never forgot Huntsman's integrity, and before he died, he made arrangements to have two people speak at his funeral: the governor of Indiana and Jon Huntsman. Apparently, Huntsman's absolute integrity made a lasting impression.

In this story, Huntsman actually lost money by choosing to be honest. But the real key is that his conscience remained intact. Like my friend on the board of directors, Huntsman chose to live his morals—his Core Values to use the language of *Launching Leaders*—in all aspects of his life. That's what gave him his peace of mind.

No matter what else happens, living a congruent life will keep you safe from the pitfalls of a segmented, duplicitous life. Remember the importance of keeping your hand on the tiller. Hang on, grip tight, and stay the course. Arriving at your destination in one piece is much more fun than letting go and fluttering in the wind. A congruent life is a life of honesty, integrity, honor, and authenticity. Staying true to your morals and your Core Values across all aspects of your life will help you keep yourself aligned with God, and the more aligned you are with God, the more abundant your life will become. In the process, you will make your mark on the world in a powerful, positive way.

Application and Relevance

1. You can't live by two sets of standards and have true success; CONGRUENCY is the key to a joyful and abundant life.

2. Duplicitous living includes everything from the big, obvious acts of lying and cheating to the small, seemingly innocent moments of dishonesty that creep into our everyday lives.

3. Hold tight to the Core Values you've established and don't sacrifice any of them on the altars of a double life.

4. Understand that living a double life will ultimately bring harm to you and to many others.

5. Choose not to live in the "gray" areas of life.

6. Decide to live a congruent life at all times and in all places, even when you're alone. Remember that the congruent life is about your outward actions as well as your inner character, values, and motives.

7. In all cases, the results of living a congruent life are:
    - Peace
    - Respect
    - Constant alignment with God
    - Untarnished reputation
    - Joy in the journey of life

Notes:

_____

_____

_____

_____

_____

_____

_____

_____

_____

_____

_____

_____

_____

_____

_____

_____

_____

_____

_____

_____

_____

CHAPTER 07

Habits of Success

"We do not act rightly because we have virtue or excellence, but
rather have those because we have acted right."

— Aristotle[32]

The water hyacinth is an aquatic plant that usually floats on the tops of fresh water ponds and lakes. The plant is considered both a pest and a blessing. On the one hand, water hyacinths multiply so quickly that they can clog irrigation systems and create micro-habitats for certain diseases. Because they're 95% water, they can also contribute to water shortages.

On the other hand, water hyacinths are known for their beautiful purplish-blue, lavender, and pink flowers. The plant's fibrous tissues can also be used to make paper, fiberboard, baskets, charcoal briquettes, fertilizers, and fish food. Because water hyacinths can be used to make so many different things, many nongovernmental organizations support programs to grow these plants as a way to bring economic activity to places that can't produce very many other goods.

Personal habits are a lot like water hyacinths. Just as the plant can be harmful or beneficial, so too will the habits you develop be either a curse or a blessing to your life. Some habits are inherently harmful and should always be avoided. Others are always beneficial and you should work to cultivate them. Still other habits can be either good or bad depending on what you do with them and how you apply them to your life. Whatever your scenario, you have the power to choose which habits you'll develop, which ones you'll break or avoid, and what you'll do with your habits. By consciously thinking about the habits you're creating, you can shape your tendencies to your good.

Work Hard To Develop The Right Habits

We can learn even more about habits by looking at the way water hyacinths grow and reproduce. A single water hyacinth can produce more than 5,000 seeds, but they also multiply by sending out short runner stems that eventually grow into new plants. If you were to put a water hyacinth into a pond, you wouldn't notice anything happening until about two weeks later. At that point, you may see a small but noticeable patch of new growth, but still nothing too substantial. By the end of the month, however, that small patch will have grown into a thick carpet of hyacinths, so much so that you won't even be able to see the water, just the beautiful green plants with blossoming flowers.

This is also how habits color our lives. We may start out with a commitment to getting up early, and for the first week or so it may be pure torture forcing ourselves to get out of bed at 5:00 a.m. At that point, it probably feels like our efforts aren't really accomplishing anything, but after a whole month of doing this it will have become a habit that's no longer a hardship and that begins adding great value and beauty to our daily lives.

In the same way that water hyacinths start off with slow, almost imperceptible growth, but then move into stages of explosive proliferation, our attempts to create new habits will initially seem like slow going. But the more you stick with it, the easier it will become until suddenly you've created a habit that produces huge changes in your life. Transformation takes time, but the results are magnificent.

When it comes to the habits that structure our daily lives, we need to consider the qualities of the water hyacinth. Like this incredible plant, we also have within us a natural instinct to grow. We want to provide goodness to the world and to those around us. We want to be looked upon as beautiful. But the water hyacinth also reminds us that we need to grow in the *right ways*, and avoid developing habits that become harmful. If we want to become truly happy people who make a positive impact on the world, we need to consciously focus on creating the habits that will produce positive growth rather than destructive obsessions or addictions. We need to develop habits that keep our best desires moving forward and that subdue our worst appetites. By harnessing the power of habits, we can bring beautiful and vibrant color into our lives. Indeed, great habits are a key piece in creating a joyful and abundant life.

Good Habits vs. Bad Habits

Since developing the right habits is so important, you need to know how to distinguish between good and bad habits. To do this, you need to think about the process of cultivating good and positive habits as a spiritual one. As you live the Cycle of Spiritual Guidance (see Chapter 1), you will become more attuned to your inner voice. Seeking out, recognizing, and listening to the inspiration of your inner voice will help you move your life in the right direction. It will also signal whether or not the habits you're creating are good or bad. When you're on a path that's aligned with God, you will feel an inner peace. When you're on the wrong path—a path that's not aligned with God—you won't have that peace and your conscience will be troubled.

The more you follow the promptings of your inner voice, the more attuned to its gentle guidance you will become. But the more you ignore the promptings of your heart, the harder it will be for you to recognize moments of inspiration. The best way to know if a habit is good or bad is to check in with your heart. Use scripture to help you determine which ideas and habits are productive and which ones aren't. Use your holy ground to pray, ponder, and meditate on the direction you're trying to head, and pay attention to what your heart tells you. Have you felt a confirmation that a particular habit or tendency will lead you down the right path, or is something you're doing troubling your conscience? Are the things you're doing and the habits you're trying to develop in line with the sacred teachings and scriptures you value most in life? Will they make it easier or harder for you to follow a positive, spiritually focused path in life?

Forming great habits that are in line with the values that matter most to you will help your journey through life become peaceful and productive. The rest of this chapter will outline four habits that will help you create the future you most desire. In the process, these habits will help you realize a more divine vision of you and your potential. Of course, you can always add new habits to your life—as long as your inner voice confirms that they're good ones—but the four habits we'll talk about below should serve as your foundation.

Four Habits To Create Your Future

Habit 1: Live what you know

Throughout this book, we've talked a lot about staying true to what you believe. All the chapters leading up to this point have made the case that one of the keys to creating a happy, meaningful, and fulfilling life is building a foundation of beliefs, morals, and values that becomes the driving factor in everything you do. This is how you imbue your daily life with purpose. It's also how you maintain alignment with God.

Hopefully at this point you've already made the decision to live a life built on such a foundation. But there's usually a fairly big gap between the moment in which we make a decision and actually following through on that decision. To ensure that your decision to live a values-driven life doesn't shrivel on the vine, you need to make a habit out of living what you know to be true. When this becomes a habit, you no longer have to think about how you'll behave in each situation you find yourself in. Instead, because you've built a habit out of living what you know, you will automatically make decisions that are in line with your values. When living this way becomes habitual, you begin building a life of integrity and congruency.

No matter where your life is at right now, making a habit out of living what you know to be right will require a change in behavior. To do this you'll need to overcome these counterproductive behaviors and tendencies first:

Counterproductive Tendency #1: Complacency

I was once talking to a college senior about some of her long-term goals. During our conversation I asked, "What are your financial aspirations and why?" While dreamily looking off into space, she replied, "I don't know. My parents established a trust fund for me when I was born—I'm not too worried about it."

Her answer indicates a type of complacency that leads to a debilitating lack of initiative or any drive to succeed. Sadly, this is a fairly common phenomenon. The authors of *Influencer: The Power to Change Anything* call this type of complacency "The Serenity Trap."[33] Sometimes when things seem like they're generally OK, it can become easy to assume that it's not really necessary for us to set goals or work hard to accomplish anything. In this state, people fall into the trap of "mistaking the edge of a rut for the horizon;" they become so settled in where they are at the moment that they fail to see the wonderful possibilities beyond their current state.

Overcoming complacency and actually living what we know to be true requires faith that there is always something better we should be striving for. It also requires that we think and act differently, that we put in the hard work to leave our comfort zones and explore other possibilities. When we begin living this way it will change us for the better. Avoiding complacency is part of aligning ourselves with God, and is a key to becoming more than we are right now.

Counterproductive Tendency #2: Immobilization

While complacency is an inherent lack of urgency or perhaps even just laziness, immobilization is driven by fear. Remember how paralyzed I was by my fear of flying? It literally froze me in my progress, and the only way to unfreeze myself was to physically move myself out of the car and into the airplane for the flying lessons that eventually helped me overcome my fears.

Fear is the opposite of faith, and faith is precisely what you need in order to make a habit out of living what you know is right. If you find yourself immobilized by fears, turn to God for the strength you need to face them and overcome them. This may also include bringing in outside help, such as a counselor, religious leader, or spiritual advisor.

Counterproductive Tendency #3: Pessimistic Attitude

Progressing in life and becoming something greater than you are right now requires that you *believe.* Instead of questioning the spiritual impressions that come to you, doubting your ability to recognize these impressions, or looking for reasons why something won't work—all of which are negative mindsets— why not first foster a positive, can-do attitude? If you start your efforts with this mindset, you're far more likely to succeed.

Make it a habit *now* to be positive about your ability to grow, change, and achieve. Focus on living your Core Values each day until doing so becomes a habit, and understand that giving way to complacency or fear will only minimize your potential and delay your transformation into the person you're capable of becoming.

Habit 2: Calibrate daily

A classic bit of folk wisdom says: "A clock is correct at least twice a day—even if it's broken." Picture a clock whose arms are frozen at 1:04. Even though it's broken, that clock will still manage to point to the correct time at two specific moments every day: 1:04 a.m. and 1:04 p.m. But for that clock to become accurate beyond just those two minutes of the day, it needs to be calibrated to a correct timepiece. The same is true in life. You can find moments of success and happiness in any number of ways, but if you want *constant* happiness, peace, and purpose you need to calibrate your life to God.

Living in alignment with God doesn't happen by accident, it happens when you intentionally work to calibrate yourself to the spiritual aspects of your life. Be willing to change, bury pride, and embrace humility. To make productive corrections to your behavior you need to review how well you do each day and be humble enough to recognize those things that need improving. Remember your Core Values, your life destinations, and your waypoints, and calibrate your life every day to the course you've charted with God.

When you work to calibrate your life daily, you acknowledge that there's always room for improvement. You also demonstrate faith that you can overcome the things that hold you back. Sometimes, calibrating yourself requires you to think differently, to move outside your comfort zone, and to change your paradigms. In *The Milkshake Moment*, Steven S. Little describes this kind of dynamic, out of the box thinking. In the book, Little explains that when he's on business trips he often likes to reward himself at the end of long days with a milkshake. He then told a story about one business trip in particular. After a long and stressful day of travel, airports, missed appointments, and delays, Little looked forward to getting back to his hotel room and decompressing with a nice, cool, refreshing vanilla milkshake. When the day was finally over and he got to his room, he immediately called room service. Here's how the conversation went:

> **Little:** *Hello, I'd like a vanilla milkshake please.*
> **Room Service:** *I'm sorry Mr. Little, but we don't have milkshakes.*
> **Little**: *All right, let me ask you this: Do you have any vanilla ice cream?*
> **Room Service**: *Yes, of course!*
> **Little**: *OK, then I'd like a full bowl of vanilla ice cream.*
> **Room Service**: *Yes sir, right away, sir. Is there anything else I can get you?*
> **Little**: *Yes, do you have any milk?*
> **Room Service**: *Yes, we have milk.*
> **Little**: *All right, here's what I'd like you to do. Please send up a tray with the full bowl of vanilla ice cream, half a glass of milk, and a long spoon. Could you do that please?*
> **Room Service**: *Certainly, right away sir.*

When his order arrived, Little poured the milk into the ice cream and mixed it all together to make the milkshake he'd been looking forward to all day.[34] The point of this story is to highlight just how easy it is to get stuck in our paradigms, and as a result, to fail to think beyond the status quo. This is exactly what happened to the room service kitchen. Stuck in their paradigm, they failed to see the obvious solution and were unable to accomplish their objectives.

In your daily calibration, you need to be adventurous enough to think differently, to challenge your assumptions and paradigms. Calibrate yourself to dynamic thinking, innovation, and passion, and away from the stagnation of the status quo. You have the ingredients you need to make a delicious milkshake, but are you like the kitchen or are you like Little? Are you blinded by ineffective paradigms or are you a dynamic thinker willing to try new things? Can you think critically enough to say to yourself: "I really need to improve on that;" "That idea didn't really work out, I need to try something different;" or "I liked the results of that action, I should do more of it?"

Sometimes the calibration process is best done in meditative and reflective moments. This is why Chapter 4 suggested starting a daily devotional in which you set aside time to study, think, ponder, meditate, and pray. Use this as your time to calibrate yourself and to keep yourself aligned with God. Think about it as a time to check in and give an accounting of your day. As you calibrate yourself to your life course and to God, there are days that you may feel a gentle, loving rebuke, a reminder in your soul that you can do better. Other times you might feel a deep sense of satisfaction, a warm "well done." In either case, taking time to regularly connect with the divine will allow you to re-calibrate yourself and get ready for another day. Make a habit out of calibrating yourself daily, and you will find yourself progressing toward your most important life goals.

Habit 3: Find hope, purpose, and gratitude

"I am fundamentally an optimist. Whether that comes from nature or nurture I cannot say. Part of being optimistic is keeping one's head pointed toward the sun, one's feet moving forward. There were many dark moments when my faith in humanity was sorely tested, but I would not and could not give myself up to despair."

— Nelson Mandela[35]

This quote from Nelson Mandela reveals his ability to see the best in any circumstance and to use that vision to move forward with purpose and faith. This is a power that lies within each of us, and if we focus on developing it the way Mandela did, it will be a powerful tool in our efforts to create lives of meaning and happiness.

Mandela's life story is definitely worth studying. He was a man of incredible strength whose convictions drove him to lead the fight against apartheid in South Africa. His activist efforts landed him in prison for 27 years. After being freed he was elected president and continued fighting for social justice until he died at the age of 95.

I wanted to start Habit 3 with Mandela's quote because it shows that the ability to maintain hope, purpose, and gratitude in whatever circumstances we find ourselves in is a powerful life habit that is *developed* and polished through adversity. Mandela explains that while his optimism was tested during the years of abuse and imprisonment he suffered under apartheid, he ultimately made a conscious decision to remain focused on whatever good he could find. Keeping himself pointed toward the sun helped him make it through even the darkest storms.

Along with Mandela, another great example of this third habit is a man named Viktor E. Frankl. Frankl was a Jewish psychiatrist from Austria who survived several Nazi death camps during World War II. After his experiences, he wrote a book called *Man's Search for Meaning*. This book went on to become hugely popular, and was listed as one of the ten most influential books in America.[36] A key theme throughout *Man's Search for Meaning* is the power of choosing to live a life filled with hope, purpose, and gratitude. As Frankl puts it:

> *"We who lived in concentration camps can remember the men who walked through the huts comforting others, giving away their last piece of bread. They may have been few in number, but they offer sufficient proof that everything can be taken from a man but one thing: the last of the human freedoms—to choose one's attitude in any given set of circumstances, to choose one's own way."*[37]

Even when you've been dealt an unfair hand in life, you can take hope in the fact that no matter what happens, you *always* have the power to choose your attitude and the way you respond to adversity. This power can become a source of strength in tough times. Make a conscious choice right now to approach life with an attitude of hope. When this attitude becomes second nature, you'll be ready to tackle whatever challenges life throws at you.

Many of Frankl's ideas grew out of a quote from the philosopher Friedrich Nietzsche: "He who has a why to live can bear almost any how."[38] This basically means that if a person has dedicated himself or herself to a clear purpose, they'll be able to withstand any circumstance they may find themselves in. Think about Mandela. He was able to survive prison and violence because he was driven by his purpose, which was to overthrow apartheid. If your life is grounded in the firm hope that things will eventually work out and get better, you always have a purpose for doing your very best, no matter what else is going on around you.

The third component of this life habit is gratitude. Being grateful is the glue that holds hope and purpose together. When you make a habit out of approaching life with an attitude of hope, and when you consciously decide to look for the good in all things, you need to take the final step of recognizing where all good things come from. We need to be grateful for whatever blessings we enjoy in the present moment, while never letting up in our quest to become better. And whatever else happens, we can always choose to be grateful simply for the chance to experience the journey of life.

The connections between hope, purpose, and gratitude become clear in a moving passage from Frankl's book. He describes what it was like to be released from a Nazi camp at the end of WWII:

> "I walked through the country past flowering meadows, for miles and miles, toward the market town near the camp. Larks rose to the sky and I could hear their joyous song. There was no one to be seen for miles around; there was nothing but the wide earth and sky and the larks' jubilation and the freedom of space. I stopped, looked around, and up to the sky—and then I went down on my knees. At that moment there was very little I knew of myself or of the world—I had but one sentence in mind—always the same: 'I called to the Lord from my narrow prison and He answered me in the freedom of space.'"[39]

Frankl and Mandela both made a habit out of finding the best in all things. By maintaining hope that things would eventually get better, they gave themselves a purpose for which to live and a reason to endure. Throughout their difficult and at times horrific experiences, they maintained a sense of gratitude that imbued their life journeys with grace and contentment—even in the face of the worst imaginable trials.

Habit 4: Celebrate victories

Early in my professional career, I frequently had to turn in reports to my boss. He used a red pen to point out my mistakes, and as a new employee I thought he was pretty harsh. After several months of this, when I was almost ready to throw in the towel, he sent back a report that said—in the same bold red ink—"Good Job." That was it. Although that note contained only two words, I was elated. Looking back on it now, the joy I felt at doing a good job was an important moment that helped launch my entire career.

It's important to recognize moments of success and celebrate your victories. I'm not saying you should be prideful or arrogant, but you should let yourself feel good about the progress you're making. As you stick to the path you've charted, take joy in reaching your waypoints. Celebrating victories will give you motivation to keep working hard, and will give you additional strength for the journey.

Throughout history, faith traditions around the world have consistently found ways to commemorate important and sacred events. Some build altars, others construct shrines, while still others erect temples, mosques, synagogues, churches, or temples. One way or another, these practices highlight the importance of marking and celebrating important events. Likewise, you should also take the time to recognize and commemorate the important moments in your life's journey by allowing yourself to celebrate your victories. Although you probably won't go out and build a temple or a shrine for yourself, you can find ways to commemorate important achievements and events in your heart. Celebrating victories in this way allows you to recognize important milestones in your life with grace, humility, and gratitude.

Sometimes, there may be a scenario when others acknowledge your victories publicly. When you receive a note of praise, a thank you, or an award, be happy and gracious. Accept praise with humility and gratitude. Think about how good it feels when your hard work is noticed and appreciated, and let this motivate you to give praise and recognition to others around you who could benefit from a victory of their own.

There are also times when the only recognition you'll receive will be a sense deep in your heart that God is aware of you. When this happens, you will be filled with joy and peace, and your heart will grow. Savor the deep sense of satisfaction, reassurance, confidence, and inner peace that comes from knowing that you are a person of worth, and let it motivate you to keep doing your best. The joy that comes from these spiritual affirmations is like a victory dance for your heart; it should give you the biggest smile of all.

Celebrating the progress you make motivates you to keep working hard. It also helps you live in the moment. Although it's important to plan ahead and thoughtfully chart your course through life, it can also become dangerous if you're always looking too far down the road and never take time to savor moments of accomplishment. So make a habit out of celebrating your victories.

Conclusion

Frankl recognized that life is not about trying to avoid challenges, trials, and hard work, but rather, about trying to use the "tension" of life to create a sense of purpose and meaning. He wrote, "What man actually needs is not a tensionless state but rather the striving and struggling for a worthwhile goal, a freely chosen task. What he needs is not the discharge of tension . . . but the call of a potential meaning waiting to be fulfilled."[40] Life is about striving, and finding joy in that striving.

Developing habits of success will give you the handholds you need to climb toward your future. The four habits we talked about in this chapter will remind you who you are and who you want to become. They will empower you to live your Core Values. If you've decided that you want to implement into your life the ideas you're learning in this book, then you've already begun mixing the concrete that will eventually become a solid foundation for everything you do. But for this concrete to actually "set" into something reliable and solid you need to *live* these principles every single day until they become habits that you don't even have to think about anymore—you just do them.

As you continue developing your true identity as a spiritual being, you will gradually begin to understand the greater purpose of your life. This greater purpose is the *why* of your life—it's *why* you live, *why* you work hard, and *why* it's important to live a life built on solid principles and values. Creating habits is the *how* of your life—the concrete means through which all of this will actually be accomplished. Your future hinges on the habits you create now. Start with the four life habits outlined in this chapter, then add on to them as needed.

Four Habits to Create Your Future

1. Live what you know

2. Calibrate daily

3. Find hope, purpose, and gratitude

4. Celebrate victories

Other Habits You'd Like to Create

Application and Relevance

1. Be sensitive to the sacred guidance of your inner voice. It will help you bury harmful habits and develop great ones.

2. To make a habit out of living what you know, focus on overcoming complacency, immobilization, and pessimism.

3. Be sure to calibrate yourself to God on a daily basis. Use your daily calibration to renew your commitment to living a dynamic life, to be courageous, to think outside the box, and to avoid falling into a rut of stagnation.

4. Make a life habit out of finding hope, purpose, and gratitude in whatever situations you find yourself in.

5. Don't get so caught up in looking down the road that you fail to live in the moment. Enjoy the journey and celebrate the victories you achieve along the way.

6. Life is about striving for greatness and taking joy in that striving.

7. Understand the WHY and the HOW of your purpose. Know what you're aiming for and how you'll get there.

8. Use the Four Habits to Create Your Future as the foundation on which other good habits will eventually be built.

9. Develop good habits and use them as the ingredients for success—it's time to make MILKSHAKES!

Notes:

_____

_____

_____

_____

_____

_____

_____

_____

_____

_____

_____

_____

_____

_____

_____

_____

_____

_____

_____

_____

_____

_____

_____

CHAPTER 08

Financial Fitness

"If you want to do good, it helps to have done well."

— Laurence Day[41]

The Parable Of The Businessman And The Fisherman

A vacationing businessman stood on the pier of a quaint fishing village in southern Mexico, watching a young fisherman pull his small boat into the dock. It was early in the afternoon. The businessman complimented the fisherman on the yellowfin tuna he'd caught.

"How long did it take you to the catch them?" the businessman asked.

"Oh, a few hours," the Mexican fisherman replied.

Then, acting out of good intentions, the businessman began questioning the fisherman's practices to see if his business expertise could be of any help. "Why don't you stay out longer and catch more fish?" he asked the young man.

"With this I have more than enough to meet my family's needs," the fisherman answered.

"But what do you do with the rest of your time?" the businessman asked him.

Responding with a warm smile, the fisherman said, "I sleep late, play with my children, watch ball games, and take siesta with my wife. Sometimes in the evenings I take a stroll into the village to see my friends, play guitar, sing, and enjoy a few drinks."

The businessman impatiently interrupted the fisherman. "Look, I have an MBA from Harvard," he said, "and I can help you be more profitable. You can start by fishing several hours longer every day. You can then sell the extra fish you catch. With the extra money, you can buy a bigger boat, and eventually several large boats."

The businessman's mind was now racing. He told the fisherman that he could help him cut out the middleman and sell directly to the processor—the fisherman could even become the processor, take control of the market, open other plants, and make millions.

"I have never thought of such things," the fisherman said when the businessman had finished. "How long will all this take?"

After a quick calculation, the businessman said, "Probably about 15-20 years. Maybe less if you work really hard."

"And then what, señor?"

"Why that's the best part!" the businessman said. "When the time is right, you can sell your company and become very rich."

"What would I do with all that money?"

The businessman told him, "You could happily retire, move to a quaint fishing village, sleep late, fish when you want, play with your grandchildren, watch ball games, and take siesta with your wife. You could stroll into the village during the evenings and enjoy singing and playing the guitar and having a few drinks with your friends."

* * * * *

I love this story. The original author of it is unknown, but it's been passed around for so many years now that it's become something of a folktale. I like this story because of how well it expresses a number of important ideas and lessons. One of the lessons this story teaches that's especially relevant to this chapter is the idea that money shouldn't become an end in and of itself.

Purpose matters, and in our world it can be very easy to get so wrapped up trying to accumulate money that we can lose sight of the bigger picture. Without even realizing it, we can drift away from life's purpose and suddenly our number one goal has become making money just for the sake of making money. Like the businessman, it is sometimes easy to become so focused on gaining wealth that we fail to see the beautiful life that's already right in front of us.

Basically, this is a story about making a living *the right way*. It's important to note that the fisherman and the businessman were both successful at making ends meet. And while it's true that one of them had clearly amassed more wealth than the other, it also seems clear that the fisherman had done a better job of keeping his greater life goals and purposes in mind. He didn't let the pursuit of money become his number one goal. Rather, his efforts to make a living enabled him to pursue the kind of life most important to him and his family.

Financial Fitness

Surely, we've all encountered the kind of ideas espoused by the businessman in this story. The world teaches us that the main thing we should focus on when it comes to our finances is simply accumulating wealth. The world tells us that making money is one of the most important things we can do, and if we don't consciously think about what we're doing, this perspective will slip in and become our perspective, too.

I know I've experienced that. There were times earlier in my life when I was driven to make money primarily out of a fear of failure. As a self-taught businessperson I often felt like a hamster running on its wheel, racing toward whatever perception of financial success I'd picked up along the way. Rather than being intentional about *why* I was working so hard to make money, I just kept running on my hamster wheel, applying whatever ideas I came across without too much thought. I didn't have a clear purpose in mind, and as a result, there were times when my only objective was to make money and grow my business. I don't think I was being greedy or doing anything bad or wrong; I just wasn't conscious or intentional about my purpose. And without a clear set of life goals driving my financial efforts, I slipped into the mindset of trying to make money simply because that's what I thought I was supposed to do.

Later in life, my family and I started a sustainable farm. I found that the time I spent working with my family and becoming a part of the earth's natural cycle was so much more fulfilling. This shift in perspective helped give me a better understanding of what true financial success looks like. Instead of getting on the hamster wheel and pursuing whatever standards of financial success we pick up from the world, the key is to find the larger meaning and purpose behind our financial activities and efforts.

We achieve true financial success when our efforts to make a living empower us to pursue worthy desires, fulfill our life goals, and navigate the course we've charted through life. And as with everything else, our financial efforts need to be aligned with our personal morals and with God if they are to become truly meaningful.

Because this definition of financial success is so different from the world's definition, we at Launching Leaders Worldwide have chosen to refer to it as "financial fitness." True financial fitness allows you to stay focused on what really matters most. Being financially fit means that, like the fisherman, you know how much is enough. It means that your financial decisions are based on your larger life goals and values, and not on any attempt to make money simply for the sake of making money.

This chapter will teach you a system for achieving financial fitness. But this system isn't a one-size-fits-all formula that you need to follow perfectly, step-by-step, exactly as it's presented. Rather, the goal of this chapter is to present you with proven principles and practices that can be applied to your life no matter what your situation is, and that will help you take charge of your finances so you can focus on what matters most.

To become truly powerful, this system needs to be tested and adjusted to meet your individual needs, demands, life goals, and Core Values. Because we're not interested solely in accumulating as much wealth as possible, the first step toward financial fitness is understanding that "success" can only be defined by your unique life circumstances, desires, and goals. This system will be most powerful when you tailor it to your individual life—taking what you need, leaving what you don't, and adapting things as needed—and when you implement it according to the inspiration and guidance of your inner voice.

Before you can begin living the real world, dollars-and-cents practices this chapter will teach you, there are a handful of important concepts and principles you need to understand first. These will give you a foundation on which you can start to craft your own personalized plan for attaining financial fitness.

5 Principles At The Foundation Of Financial Fitness

1. Maintain A Healthy Perspective

When it comes to how you view material things, you need to be consciously aware of your *perspective*. Will money change you and the way you see the world? Will it alter the way you view your fellow human beings? Will you be able to keep your priorities straight in the face of material success? Will you continue focusing on your spiritual health and your connection with the divine? Will your possessions destroy you or will you use your financial self-sufficiency to build up those around you? Will you become arrogant and self-centered or will you remain humble?

In all your financial endeavors, always remember that you are part of something that extends far beyond yourself. You are connected to those around you and to the entire human family. You live in a massive universe, and yet are linked to a higher power. Nothing you do happens in a vacuum. Maintaining a humble perspective focused on the realization that you are one part of a vast and infinitely beautiful tapestry of life will help ensure that your financial desires or successes do not pull you away from the path you've charted through life. The best way to approach financial fitness is with a humble attitude, committed to using whatever blessings you receive to make a positive impact in the lives of all within your reach.

2. Know Your Context

A key part of learning how to effectively manage your money is being aware of your context. Millennials around the world are dealing with a very different economy than previous generations. To succeed, you need to be aware of the unique challenges and opportunities this economy presents, and then tailor the concepts and skills you learn in this book to meet them.

Some of the most significant factors, trends, and realities defining the economy in which Millennials are entering adulthood and launching their careers are:

- An increasingly globalized marketplace
- A focus on technology and digital connectivity
- High unemployment rates
- Dropping wages
- Rising costs of education

Some of these factors present many new opportunities, while others present a variety of new obstacles. And of course, some of these factors are more pronounced in certain places than others, and not all factors will affect everybody equally. But by and large, Millennials around the world are facing a unique economy in which it's becoming increasingly difficult for 20- and 30-somethings to make a good living.

According to Brandee McHale, president of Citi Foundation, there are 4.6 million Millennials currently without jobs in the United States. But, she points out, "this isn't just a U.S. trend. Cities and countries around the world are grappling with ways to help move their young people towards economic success. This is important because right now, approximately 75 million [Millennials] globally are actively seeking meaningful employment."[42]

This information isn't intended to scare you or to discourage you. It's intended to help you become aware of the context in which you live so that you can understand how best to tackle it. To be sure, you live in a time when the economic headwinds are blowing especially hard against you, but the good news is that there are still principles you can apply that will empower you to make progress in even the most challenging circumstances.

Try to understand and confront the full picture of your reality, and then use what you're learning in this book to help you move forward with purpose, faith, and power. Seek out mentors who are savvy to the current economic situation and who are willing to share their expertise and insight with you. As you set long-term goals and short-term waypoints, be sure they make sense in the context of your reality. Test out the principles and practices of financial fitness outlined in this chapter and tailor them to your unique circumstances, needs, and goals. And throughout it all, keep yourself aligned with God.

Rather than being afraid of today's economic realities, let your full awareness of them empower you to make smart decisions, set meaningful goals, seek out relevant mentors, and make plans to move forward armed with faith and knowledge.

3. Be A Good Steward

The word "stewardship" has a sacred ring to it. Good stewardship has to do with living a particular set of ethics, and requires that we responsibly plan for and manage the resources under our care. One of the key principles on which financial fitness is based is the idea that we are responsible for being good stewards of our material blessings. We need to take good care of whatever material possessions we acquire in life. We should never take things for granted. And most importantly, we should seek to use whatever wealth we attain for good.

As I was thinking about what being a good financial steward might mean for Millennials, I decided to ask one of my Millennial-aged sons for his thoughts.

I found his perspective to be both inspired and refreshing:

The idea of stewardship and giving back are concepts that many Millennials consider to be top priorities. The perspectives we have on these things are very different from those of past generations.

Millennials are often characterized as a "lost" or an "entitled" generation. This is a gross misrepresentation of a generation that actually cares a lot about helping others and striving to craft an egalitarian society. In the past, it was entirely possible—and even probable—that a person could count on an employer's loyalty during good times and bad, as long as that person worked diligently and with integrity. This is no longer the case for most Millennials. The working world has changed and so Millennials have had to change along with it.

Many of us Millennials in the United States and throughout the world spent our formative years watching a booming period of success. We saw our parents work hard and achieve their goals. Many of our parents were able to buy homes, cars, and other goods. In some cases, our parents achieved high levels of material wealth.

But in the midst of all this success, Millennials also saw that their parents' happiness didn't necessarily increase because they made more than enough to cover their basic needs and a few wants. We saw our parents work hard to provide for their families and to succeed, but we also noticed that they had little time to actually just be in the same room with their kids. Later on, after they made money and accumulated all sorts of toys, the world economy almost collapsed and we watched our parents—many of whom were loyal workers and employees—be treated very poorly by their employers. Many of our parents lost their jobs and the careers they'd devoted their entire lives to building were suddenly over.

What all this means is that there's more than meets the eye when it comes to Millennials. Most of us don't view ourselves as entitled, but rather as people for whom being treated like an equal is of the utmost importance. It's telling that, in a technologically advanced world, Millennials would rather trade their time and money to have meaningful experiences—whether offline or online—than for big homes and fancy cars. There is a movement among many in our generation toward simplification. This is both of necessity, due to the difficult job market we're entering, and because we've already seen from our parents' lives that owning as much stuff as possible doesn't actually lead to happiness.

Because of all this, many Millennials view the typical corporate career track with a measure of skepticism that previous generations didn't really have. If you try to put Millennials on the hamster wheel of making money and climbing the corporate ladder, you'd better be prepared to also explain to them specifically what's in it for them. This is often misinterpreted as selfishness, but Millennials want to know "what's in it for them" because they saw so many of the promises made to their parents eventually be broken. This is wisdom not selfishness.

For many of us, the perspective is not "save money for 30 years and then share it with others." Instead, it's "make money, save a little, and share along the way as often as we can."

From what I can tell, many Millennials are already looking for something that goes beyond simply making money for the sake of making money. As my son described it, they're primarily concerned with quality of life, making connections with others, having meaningful experiences, and creating a more livable society. This perspective is exactly what it means to be a good steward. Living this principle means you're making money for the right reasons, and that you're maintaining a healthy perspective that's grounded in a sincere desire to do good.

4. Prepare For Rainy Day Peace

Self-reliance is another fundamental principle of financial fitness. When you think about your finances in terms of self-reliance you shift your focus away from trying to simply accumulate wealth and instead focus on building a security net for you and your loved ones that will bring real peace of mind. And because all aspects of our lives are interconnected—remember the importance of congruency from Chapter 6—the principle of self-reliance applies equally whether we're talking about personal or business finances.

One cold fall night back in 2008, as the economic recession was really starting to hit, I received a phone call from a friend. I'd just finished some meetings for the day and was immediately struck by the panicked tone of my friend's voice. As soon as I picked up, he told me that the assets in his retirement account had just lost close to 50% of their value over the course of a day or two. He asked if he should sell what was left.

Unfortunately, this wasn't my only friend who was feeling that way. After our conversation ended, I began questioning myself. When so many people I knew were suddenly in panic mode, why was I still feeling so calm? Was I missing something? Was I being too simple-minded to fully understand what was going on? Should I be panicking more than I was?

As my mind raced through these questions, I realized that one part of why I wasn't feeling as anxious as many others was because the sector in which my business operated was not as adversely affected by market swings as many other businesses were. But beyond that, I realized that the biggest reason I wasn't feeling too anxious was because Ginger and I had already structured our finances around a set of common sense, spiritually-informed principles that had allowed us to build a wall of protection against rainy days like this. Because we'd prepared ourselves, we had peace in the midst of the storms.

Of course, we still suffered financial setbacks during this period, but because we'd planned our finances according to the principles and practices outlined in this chapter, we weathered the turbulence just fine. I believe that one of the most important reasons to work hard to become financially fit is to prepare for rainy days. This preparation will give you a unique and powerful sense of safety and security, something I like to call "Rainy Day Peace."

5. Be a Lifelong Learner

Making an effort to acquire as much knowledge as possible is truly a key to becoming financially fit. The more you know about finances, money management, and investing, the more effective all your financial endeavors will become. This chapter is an excellent starting place, but don't stop here. Continue learning throughout your life so that you can become a truly great steward of your material blessings.

To accomplish this, make a conscious effort to get advice from wise men, women, and other resources that will help you become well educated in the management of your money. As we talked about in Chapter 3, seek out great mentors who can show you the ropes and share helpful insights with you. Read the best books, watch the best shows, follow the best blogs, and listen to the best podcasts. Do whatever you can to learn, grow, and hone your skills.

In your efforts to become a lifelong learner, remember the importance of context. Understand that the financial and economic realities of your generation are much different than those of previous generations. The headwinds blowing against you are stronger, which means that to succeed you need to learn how to apply sound financial principles in a way that's appropriate to your context. That's why you need to use this chapter as your starting place, and then continue expanding your knowledge by seeking out mentors and other sources—just be sure that they are explicitly aware of the specific context in which Millennials live and work.

Finally, as you pursue knowledge and learning, watch out for wolves in sheep's clothing. Be wary of mentors whose interest in you is tied more to multiplying their own fortunes than in graciously sharing their wisdom and success with you as a friend. Similarly, look out for self-proclaimed financial gurus who promise to teach you how to gain financial success if you pay them lots of money to buy into their system. Certainly, professionals in the financial services industry need to make a living, and paying them for their expertise is fine. Just be careful that you're getting sound advice at an affordable price, and not being taken advantage of. To discern between good and bad advice, wise and dangerous teachers, listen to the divine guidance of your inner voice. And if somebody presents you with a fabulous financial opportunity with huge expected returns, but that requires you to act under a high pressure, super tight deadline, run like the wind. In everything you do, be smart and wise.

If you focus on keeping your financial decisions aligned with a healthy perspective, strive to be a good steward of your material belongings, frame your finances in terms of self-reliance, and work to become a lifelong learner, you'll be well on your way toward achieving financial fitness. With these principles in mind, let's turn to the concrete practices that will allow you to put these principles to work. As you read, keep in mind that these practices can be followed exactly as they're presented here, or they can be adapted and revised to better meet your unique needs, goals, and life circumstances. If you feel unfamiliar with finances, you might want to begin by following these steps pretty closely and then make adjustments as you become more comfortable and confident. As with everything else, the key is to seek and follow spiritual guidance as you strive to achieve your goals and travel the course you've charted through life.

Achieving Financial Fitness: A Step-by-Step Guide

The fields of finance and finance management have become so wrapped up in confusing jargon that it can sometimes seem like the only way to manage your money is to hire an expensive financial planner. All that confusion ends up deterring people from learning how to take charge of their finances, and as a result, very few people manage their money smartly or effectively.

One of the most powerful aspects of the system you're about to learn is that it gives you a straightforward, understandable, and actionable approach to managing your finances. Keeping it simple works, as long as you're committed to the process and are willing to work hard, make some sacrifices, and have self-discipline. This system is the model my wife and I have followed throughout our marriage, and it's allowed us to launch a business, stay out of debt, pay for our living expenses, fund a comfortable retirement, and have a little fun along the way.

Before we get started, a quick note: This system requires you to set up one checking account and three savings accounts. It's important that these accounts are set up separately and that they're never co-mingled. If all the money you make were to go into one pot, it would become very difficult to track precisely where your money is going, to implement your plans, and to attain your financial goals. But putting your funds into separate and clearly defined accounts gives you a built-in system for disciplined spending and saving. With all that said, let's dive in.

Step 1: Don't Just Work Hard—Work Productively

Hard work is a wonderful thing; there's a reason why it's the first step in both The Formula and this chapter's model of financial fitness. Without hard work, they would both fall flat.

As you strive to work hard, it's important to look for a line of work that you enjoy. I'm not saying you need to have a perfect job—in fact, I've never actually seen such a thing in real life. But you should find a job that allows you to do something you enjoy. As Steve Jobs said, "Your work is going to fill a large part of your life, and the only way to be truly satisfied is to do what you believe is great work. And the only way to do great work is to love what you do. If you haven't found it yet, keep looking. Don't settle. As with all matters of the heart, you'll know when you find it."[43]

Doing something that you love will help you work hard and will allow you to find meaning in what you do, but simply putting forth a lot of effort isn't what truly effective work is all about. Working hard and expending a lot of energy don't necessarily mean you're being *productive*. That's what Henry Ford discovered when he conducted a survey in 1926 and found that shortening the work week from six days down to five actually increased productivity.[44] I call this phenomenon "unstringing the bow." In archery, if you leave your bow strung all the time, the bowstring will eventually lose its elasticity, the bow will lose its flex, and the entire thing becomes useless. Humans operate a lot like bows. Robert Taft recognized this when he said: "Only the man able to rest and relax, to laugh and play, will be able to fight and struggle, lead and guide. Only the man who knows when he has come to the end of his energy will be able to expend even greater energy."[45]

As you focus on not just working hard, but working *productively*, remember the 80/20 Rule. This rule states that 20% of our effort produces 80% of the results. To get the most out of your efforts and to be as productive as possible, you need to focus your energy on those things that produce the greatest results. To do this, you may need to delegate some of your responsibilities. You may need to swallow your pride and ask more questions so that you can learn better ways of doing things. Avoid repetitive tasks that can be automated, don't be so much of a perfectionist that every task takes forever to complete, try to make your decisions based on more data and less guess work, and don't drive yourself so hard that you burn out. Learn the difference between working hard and being productive, and strive to ensure that the hard work you perform produces the best results.

Step 2: Pay Yourself First—The Independence Account

In his groundbreaking book *The Richest Man in Babylon*, George S. Clason coined the phrase, "A part of all you earn is yours to keep."[46] The basic idea behind this phrase is that in order to achieve financial independence and self-reliance you must pay yourself first. But we're not talking about paying yourself so you can go out and spend frivolously. What we're talking about is setting aside a portion of everything you earn for a savings account that's been specifically designated as your Independence Account. The money you deposit into your Independence Account is to be used only for making investments.

While the specific ins and outs of investing are beyond the scope of this book, part of your efforts to be a good steward and a lifelong learner should include learning as much as you can about how to become a savvy investor. Start simple with things like establishing a 401K, opening a Roth IRA, and taking advantage of any retirement funds your employer might offer, and then work your way up into other types of investments.

As you eventually begin moving money out of your Independence Account and into actual investments, you start building your Gold Fund. Whatever returns your investments make stay in the Gold Fund and are reinvested. The whole idea is that you never touch any of this money until the day that the interest, dividends, and profits your investments make are enough to pay all of your living expenses.

Because you're always contributing to your Independence Account, you'll always have funds available for investing. When it's done right, the Independence Account is what really gets the ball of financial independence rolling. Setting up and contributing to an Independence Account that in turn feeds the investments in your Gold Fund will allow you to really put your money to work. When you pay yourself first and then invest those funds, your money will start generating even more money until you eventually become self-reliant. The Independence Account is where it all starts.

Step 3: Plan To Give Charitably

In your efforts to be a good steward, consider making charitable donations a regular part of your financial plan. Throughout this book, we've talked about the importance of making a positive impact and giving back. When you make giving a standard part of your pathway to financial fitness, you ensure that you're always giving to others—it becomes an automatic part of how you manage your money. Many people of faith end up deciding to donate a predetermined percentage of their income even before they pay their Independence Accounts. However you choose to do it, a key part of becoming financially fit is using your money as a way of giving back and serving others. This will help you keep your financial activities directly aligned with a giving oriented, well-balanced perspective.

Step 4: Establish A Budget And Stick To It

For this step, you need to set up a checking account that you will use to pay for your regular day-to-day expenses. This includes things like food, rent, utilities, cell phone, and any other bills that are part of your everyday life.

The key to managing this account is setting up a budget. You need to keep track of the money you have coming in and the expenses you have going out. When you first try to figure out how much it will cost you to live each month, there will be a lot of guesswork, so you'll need to make adjustments as you go. But ultimately, you'll want an accurate calculation of how much your regular living expenses should be each month. This budget will help you keep track of where your money goes and will help you know if you're spending more than you can afford. Budgets can be powerful because they allow you to actively guide where your money goes rather than simply wonder where it went.

But budgets only work if you stick to them. If you know that your monthly income will allow you to spend only a certain amount on food each month, and then you ignore your budget by going out to eat at expensive restaurants every weekend, you've just thrown your finances all out of balance. In order to make up for the extra money you spent on food, you'll have to pull funds from some other part of your budget or put it all on your credit card and go into debt. Both options will keep you from moving forward toward financial fitness and self-reliance.

The key to sticking to your budget is to live on less than you make. If you're struggling to keep your budget, you need to adjust either your expenses or your income. Getting your budget squared away is paramount to moving forward with success. Frugal living allows you to avoid debt and maybe even be able to put a little bit extra into your Independence Account. But don't get too carried away with all this; don't let your budget rule your life or make you miserable. Be sure you give yourself some freedom to spend money on things that you enjoy. Just don't go into debt or make decisions that will derail your efforts to achieve financial fitness. As Clason puts it: "Enjoy life while you are here. Do not overstrain or try to save too much."[47] Establishing a budget and sticking to it will help you take charge of your money by consciously controlling how much goes toward which expenses.

Step 5: Create a Savings Account For Non-Regular Expenses

Saving is an important practice when it comes to your stewardship of money. It's the key to financial discipline, it's what allows you to prepare for rainy days, and it's what enables you to make constant, uninterrupted progress toward financial independence. Saving really is the key to surviving in both good times and bad times. Building up your storehouse is a powerful principle that will allow you to sleep well even when the wind blows.

But saving isn't just about surviving—it's about thriving. When you save, you'll be able to take advantage of opportunities that you might not otherwise be able to. In 2008, when the real estate market took a nosedive, those who had saved up were able to buy homes for pennies on the dollar. By 2015, these homes had become massive cash flow producers thanks to record high rental rates.

While the concept of saving is present in every step of this model for financial fitness, it's most pronounced in this one. After you pay yourself by contributing to your Independence Account, make some sort of meaningful donation, and budget out your regular expenses, you need to set aside some money for unexpected expenses. These non-regular expenses might be taxes, medical surprises, a broken down car, the cost of moving to a new city, or anything else that might suddenly pop up. Some of these expenses can be accurately budgeted, but many are entirely unexpected. If you don't have a savings account ready to handle these surprise expenses, one emergency can suddenly derail your entire effort to become financially fit. But if you save in advance for these types of unplanned expenses, you won't have to rob any other accounts to pay for them. Don't shortchange this savings account; plan on adding at least a small portion of your income to it every time you get paid.

Step 6: Contribute to Your Wish List Account

Being a good, smart, and responsible steward of your money doesn't mean you can't derive any enjoyment out of the money you earn. In fact, using money just for fun is an important part of financial fitness. This is what helps you avoid becoming so uptight about your finances that you inadvertently become a slave to your savings accounts and investments. But, of course, if your fun spending goes unchecked, it can seriously slow down your progress toward self-reliance.

Contributing a portion of your income to a savings account devoted specifically to fun spending is the best way to find the right balance of enjoying what you earn while not getting too carried away. A wish list account works best if you add to it only after you've paid yourself first, made some sort of charitable donation, budgeted out your regular expenses, and set aside a little bit for unexpected rainy days. At that point, all your bases are covered and you can feel free to save up for something fun. This might be a new car, recreational equipment, a big vacation, or any other thing you dream of doing or owning. A good example of how to use a wish list account would be to set aside a little bit each month until you've built up enough to buy a new car with cash. This will allow you to avoid ever having to pay interest, which really is the bill that never sleeps.

How It All Works

To see how all these steps might work together in the real world, let's look at one possible scenario. Before we dive into the numbers, though, let me be clear that this is just a model. To see how all the steps I've just outlined might apply to you specifically, you'd need to adjust the following model to account for your particular situation. For example, the model below does not include paying off debt from student loans. For many Millennials this is a significant financial concern. If this, or any other variable, applies to you, be sure you adjust your estimates and calculations appropriately. You may need to increase the amount you budget out for regular expenses in order to account for things like student loan payments, which will obviously affect all the other figures.

With that said, our general model will assume that your monthly net pay (after taxes have been taken out) is $2,500. Let's say you've decided to pay your Independence Account 10% of your net income, which means that every month you put $250 into that savings account. Let's say you've also committed to donating 10% of your net income to a charitable cause that's important to you. That's another $250 every month. You've budgeted out $1,450 per month for your regular expenses, $300 for your non-regular expenses, and your last $250 for your wish list account. Here's what it looks like on paper:

Monthly View: Income $2,500 (after taxes)

Independence account, pay yourself first; a part of what you earn is yours to keep!
$250

Give back, make giving back a regular part of your stewardship.
$250

Budget account for regular living expenses.
$1,450

Savings account for non-regular expenses not calculated in the budget account.
$300

Savings account for wish list.
$250

If you stuck with this plan for one year, the totals would look like this:

Year One Totals: Income $30,000 (after taxes)

Independence account, pay yourself first; a part of what you earn is yours to keep!
$3,000

Give back, make giving back a regular part of your stewardship.
$3,000

Budget account for regular living expenses.
$17,400

Savings account for non-regular expenses not calculated in the budget account.
$3,600

Savings account for wish list.
$3,000

Note that your Independence Account already has a whopping $3,000 ready for you to invest. This is where the fun begins. That $3,000 will become the snowball that eventually creates an avalanche of financial independence. As you start moving money out of your Independence Account and into actual investments, you've officially started building your Gold Fund, the source of income that will one day make your financial independence possible.

To think about the Gold Fund it can be helpful to compare it to the well-known fable of the goose that laid the golden eggs. In an effort to get rich quick, the couple in the story killed the goose thinking they could get all the gold out of the goose's body at once. They were dismayed to discover that wasn't the case; the goose's insides were just the same as any other goose.

Because of their impatience, the characters in the story killed the goose that laid the golden eggs. This is a good lesson for how to approach your Gold Fund. Although there will be times when it may not seem like it, investing the money in your Independence Account truly is your best chance to make the most of what you've saved up. Smart investing is what will turn your Independence Account into your own personal golden egg-laying goose, but it will only work if you're patient and if you continue working productively, learning from good financial mentors, and if you let time do its work.

In so many ways, time is one of the most important keys to being successful in your financial endeavors. Despite fluctuations in the stock market, good investing will almost definitely yield profits *in the long run.* Similarly, an investment that accrues interest picks up momentum, earning more and more interest, the *longer* your money remains invested. Use this knowledge to your benefit and don't be like the couple in the story. Let time do its work, and slowly but surely, the little bit you put into your Independence Account will transform itself into a pile of golden eggs.

As you begin making dividends, interest, and returns on your investments, don't just take out your earnings and spend them. Instead, reinvest them back into the market. In this way, your earnings will grow exponentially, at an ever-increasing rate, until you can pay for all your expenses strictly on the profits you earn from your investments. This is the point at which you've achieved financial independence. When you reach this point, your money generates enough money all on its own that you no longer have to rely on working a steady job to maintain your lifestyle.

In its simplest form, here is what an Independence Account looks like:

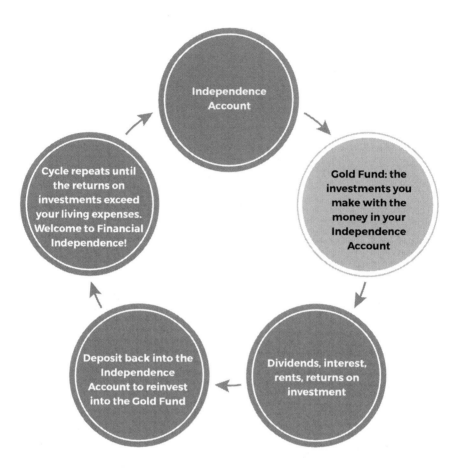

This entire cycle starts by contributing a portion of your income to the Independence Account, and then making sure that all your other expenses are budgeted out and accounted for so that you never have to dip into the money you're saving up to invest.

To really demonstrate the power of an Independence Account, let's take a look at a real world example. Suppose you saved up enough in your Independence Account for a $20,000 down payment on a rental property that costs $100,000. After calculating out all the expenses of owning the property, you figure that it will cost you a little less than $8,000 a year to maintain. But since you can rent the property for $1,250 a month you know you've got a winner. Here are all the numbers on paper, and remember, these are all just estimates to demonstrate how the Independence Account can help you build up a lucrative Gold Fund:

Estimates of Rental Home Costs and Expenses

Purchase Price: $100,000

Down Payment: $20% of $100,000 = $20,000 (this comes straight from Independence Account.) Note: Many lenders will allow less money down, which will change the rest of the numbers. Again, this is just a model.

30 Year Mortgage @ 4% = $447.42 Monthly Payment.

Annual estimated costs: Insurance ($500.00) + Taxes ($600.00) + Maintenance fees ($1,200) = $2,300 per year or $191.67 per month.

Summary: After making the $20,000 down payment, the property will cost you $7,669.04 per year to maintain. That's $639.08 a month.

Now that we've added up all our estimated costs and expenses, let's see what the property would bring in:

Estimates of Rental Home Income

Monthly Rental Rate: $1,250 per month = $15,000 per year

Vacancy Rate = 1 month per year = $1,250 per year

Yearly income from rents: $15,000 (monthly rate) - $1,250 (vacancy rate) = $13,750

Yearly income from rents ($15,000) - yearly costs and expenses ($7,669.04) = yearly net income of $7,330.96

Again, these are just very rough estimates, but if this were an actual investment property, the returns it produces would be considered very good all around. As your profits start coming in on this rental, you'd put them straight back into your Independence Account, which will continue growing until you're ready for your next investment. If this process continues with similar returns on other investments, your Gold Fund will eventually provide the income you need to sustain yourself without ever having to touch the principal. Ideally, this becomes a fully self-sustaining cycle that will carry you to the point of financial independence.

Keep in mind that while all this is going on, you're still working your job, budgeting out your expenses, and contributing to your various accounts. By following this system, you've become a good steward of your finances. You know where all your money goes every month, you've got all your expenses covered, you're giving back on a regular basis, preparing for emergencies, and giving yourself the freedom to have fun along the way—all while using your Independence Account to create a continually growing nest egg.

Some Final Notes

As one final thought, I'd like to turn quickly to the concept of sustainability. As I mentioned earlier in this chapter, my family and I own a sustainable farm. We work together to raise our own produce, chickens, eggs, cows, sheep, pigs, and ducks—pretty much everything on Old McDonald's farm.

We have two main objectives for our farm. The first is to provide for as many of our family's needs as possible, so we don't have to rely on going to the store for the goods we need. The second objective is to eventually move from being just self-sustaining to the point that we can earn a profit from our farm that can be reinvested into our Gold Fund. To show you how this second objective might look, here's a simple example having to do with chickens. For this example, let's say we had a chicken coop with six chickens.

Sustainable Egg Business

Cost of Chicken Coop and six hens: $150.00

Egg production at peak = 5 eggs per hen per week or 30 eggs total.

Eggs selling for $5.00 per dozen = $12.50 per week; $54.00 per month average.

In this simple model, the initial $150 investment would be paid for in three months, and everything on top of that could then be invested into our Gold Fund. Note that this model assumes that the chickens are pasture raised, in which case there are minimal costs for feeding them. In just one year, we'd be able to put close to $500 into our fund to be used for future investments.

Alternatively, we could eat the eggs and save the money we would have normally spent buying eggs in the store. Either way, it's a winner.

There are two main principles I'd like to focus on here. The first has to do with sustainability. Note that in the paragraph above, I said that our *first* priority is providing for our needs. Only after our basic needs are met can we move onto our *second* objective, which is making a profit. In your own life, it doesn't make any sense to try and plan ahead for the future if you're already drowning in the present. If you're not making ends meet, you need to make an adjustment to how much you're spending—you may need to tighten your budget—or to how much you're making—you may need to find a better paying job or take on a second job to accomplish this. One way or another, being a good steward means that you're providing for your basic needs first and foremost. The beauty of the six-step plan I've just presented to you is that it gives you a way to provide for all your needs while also preparing for the future at the same time.

The second lesson I want to highlight from my experiences with our sustainable farm is the power of starting where you are. As long as you're providing for your basic needs, don't feel like you have to wait until you have some massive income to start saving, or a huge lump of cash before you start investing. Even if all you have is a couple dozen of eggs to sell every week, that's enough to get the ball rolling. Wherever you're at with your finances, now is the time to take charge. Start managing your money, controlling how you spend it, and setting aside even a little bit for your Independence Account. You'll be surprised how things start to add up month after month, and year after year. If you're currently in debt, include your payments into your budget for regular expenses, and adjust everything else so you can still pay your Independence Account—even if the amount you can contribute each month seems small and inconsequential.

When my wife, Ginger, and I first started this system, our funds were so tight that we could only add a tiny amount to our Independence Account after paying for everything else. But we stayed at it and five years later, we were able to start putting our little savings account to work. Since that time, our small nest egg has grown to become a key piece in the financial independence we enjoy today. Those first five years really flew by, and although it didn't seem like we were accomplishing very much, our attempts to live within our means, to sacrifice, and to live with purpose and intention really added up. If you're like we were, and you feel like you can't figure out how to stay afloat, much less save and plan, then consider the power of time. Start right where you are, and watch as your efforts today yield surprisingly huge results down the road. But the key is to actually get the process started, to get that first tiny snowball rolling down the hill. Be sure you're taking care of your basic needs, and start saving and planning today, right where you are.

In Summary

The ideas and practices presented in this chapter give you a sound and proven approach to managing your money effectively. But remember that the goal is *financial fitness*, not simply making money for the sake of making money or trying to get rich for the sake of getting rich. You need to figure out exactly what financial fitness means to you, and how it might fit in with your life goals, your Core Values, and the course you've charted for yourself. The whole point is to use the ideas in this chapter to tailor a system that works for you.

However you choose to define and pursue financial fitness, I hope the material in this chapter helps you get there. Ultimately, I hope that your approach to financial fitness allows you to happily retire to a quaint coastal fishing village, sleep late, fish when you want, play with your grandchildren, watch ball games, take siesta with your mate, stroll into the village in the evenings to enjoy singing and playing the guitar and having a few drinks with your friends—if this is your desire. Whatever your desires are, I hope that the way you manage your money gives you a deep sense of peace and security that will allow you to pursue whatever it is that matters most to you.

Application and Relevance

1. Financial fitness isn't about getting rich, it's about managing your money so that you can accomplish your life goals and become the type of person you're capable of becoming.

2. Always remember the source from which all blessings flow.

3. However you choose to apply them, the principles at the foundation of financial fitness are:
   a. Maintain a healthy perspective
   b. Know your context
   c. Be a good steward
   d. Prepare for Rainy Day Peace
   e. Be a lifelong learner

4. Become familiar with this chapter's six-step system for achieving financial fitness, and then adapt it to meet the specific needs, circumstances, and goals of your unique life.

5. The step-by-step model for becoming financially fit:
   Step 1. Don't just work hard—work *productively.*
   Step 2. Pay yourself first by depositing a portion of your income into your Independence Account.
   Step 3. Consider making charitable donations a regular part of your financial activity.
   Step 4. Establish a budget and stick to it; use your checking account to cover these regular expenses.
   Step 5. Create a savings account that will help you survive those unexpected "rainy day" expenses.
   Step 6. Contribute to your wish list savings account.

6. As soon as you've saved up enough in your Independence Account, start investing it to create your Gold Fund. Keep any returns, interests, and profits your investments make in your Gold Fund, ready for your next investment. Follow this pattern until your investments make enough to cover your living expenses. This is financial independence.

7. If you're managing your money effectively, you should be able to cover your basic needs while also preparing for the future. Start where you are and take charge of your finances. Money should become a tool enabling you to pursue whatever it is that matters most to you in life, not an end in and of itself.

Notes:

_____

_____

_____

_____

_____

_____

_____

_____

_____

_____

_____

_____

_____

_____

_____

_____

_____

_____

_____

_____

_____

CHAPTER 09

Rise Above and Make a Difference

"An individual has not started living until he can rise above the narrow confines of his individualistic concerns to the broader concerns of all humanity."

— Martin Luther King, Jr. [48]

Up to this point, this book has shared with you a number of principles, ideas, formulas, and suggestions, all of which have been aimed at helping you maximize your potential, discover true happiness and meaning, and bring *your* vision into alignment with a more divine and boundless vision of who you are and what you can become. A lot of what's been said so far requires you to push yourself out of your comfort zone. But this begs the question, why stretch your limits this way? Why do these things that might be difficult, uncomfortable, and maybe even a little bit scary? What is the value of pushing yourself to become more than you already are? What is really the point of doing all this anyway?

Perhaps some of these questions have already been answered in earlier chapters. But in this section of the book, we want to suggest that one of the most important reasons for working hard to rise above mediocrity to become your best possible self is because this is how you'll make the biggest impact on the world around you. As you maximize your potential, sharpen your skills, stay true to what you know, and align yourself with God, you are being shaped for a cause that extends beyond yourself. Moving above and beyond mediocrity is the path to discovering the most rewarding purpose of all: making a positive impact.

Throughout my observations of life, I've noticed that every single person seems to have a need to love and be loved, and a desire to make some sort of a difference. These needs and desires seem to be almost innate. We see this in young children who, when a new sibling joins the family, need to be reassured that they're still known and loved. We see this in the aging, who wonder how long their lives will be seen as relevant and important. These yearnings for love and the desire to be a valuable presence in someone else's life never end.

Making a positive, meaningful impact in the lives of those around us is truly the hallmark of a successful and abundant life. It's what allows us to become more than just self-interested, self-serving individuals. It's what helps us connect with others and fill our lives with love, belonging, and community. It's what gives us a powerful sense of purpose and meaning that will both motivate us to live well and fill us with a deep-seated sense of happiness, peace, and contentment.

Small Things Make A Huge Difference

Whenever we talk about making a positive impact on the world, it's easy to fall into the trap of thinking that the only efforts that really count are the big, dramatic, publicly visible ones. Stories about wealthy philanthropists or celebrities donating millions of dollars to charitable causes quickly come to mind, and we can easily start to assume that this kind of giving is the only way to really, truly make a difference.

But we need to keep in mind that every effort is valuable, meaningful, and hugely important. The scale or size of one's giving isn't what matters. What matters is that we use our talents and blessings to their fullest, devoting ourselves to walking a life path that's grounded in spirituality and love. When we do this, we will most certainly find ways to make a positive and meaningful impact on the world around us. As you strive to do this, keep in mind that small things really do make a huge difference. To illustrate this point, here's one of my favorite stories from William J. Bennett's *The Book of Virtues*:[49]

King Richard the Third was preparing for the fight of his life. An army led by Henry, Earl of Richmond, was marching against him. The contest would determine who would rule England. The morning of the battle, Richard sent a groom to make sure his favorite horse was ready.

"Shoe him quickly," the groom told the blacksmith. "The King wishes to ride at the head of his troops."

"You'll have to wait," the blacksmith answered. "I've shoed the king's whole army the last few days, and now I've got to go get more iron."

"I can't wait," the groom shouted impatiently. "The king's enemies are advancing, and we must meet them on the field. Make do with what you have."

So the blacksmith bent to his task. From a bar of iron he made four shoes. He hammered and shaped and fitted them to the horse's feet. Then he began to nail them on. But after he had fastened three shoes, he found he did not have enough nails for the fourth.

"I need one or two more nails," he said, "and it will take some time to hammer

them out."

"I told you I can't wait," the groom said impatiently. "I hear the trumpets now. Can't you just use what you've got?"

"I can put the shoe on, but it won't be as secure as the others."

"Will it hold?" asked the groom.

"It should," answered the blacksmith, "but I can't be certain."

"Well, then, just nail it on," the groom cried, "And hurry, or King Richard will be angry with us both."

The armies clashed, and Richard was in the thick of the battle. He rode up and down the field, cheering his men and fighting his foes.

"Press forward! Press forward!" he yelled, urging his troops toward Henry's lines.

Far away, at the other end of the field, he saw some of his men falling back . . . So Richard spurred his horse and galloped toward the broken line, calling on his soldiers to turn and fight.

He was barely halfway across the field when one of the horse's shoes flew off. The horse stumbled and fell, and Richard was thrown to the ground. Before the king could grab at the reins, the frightened animal rose and galloped away. Richard looked around him. He saw that his soldiers were turning and running, and Henry's troops were closing around him.

He waved his sword in the air. "A horse!" he shouted. "A horse! My kingdom for a horse!"

But there was no horse for him. His army had fallen to pieces, and his troops were busy trying to save themselves. A moment later Henry's soldiers were upon Richard, and the battle was over.

And since that time, people have said,

For want of a nail, a shoe was lost,
For want of a shoe, a horse was lost,
For want of a horse, a battle was lost,
For want of a battle, the kingdom was lost,
And all for the want of a horseshoe nail.

As you consider the ways you can make a positive difference in the world, remember that every effort counts. Out of seemingly little things, truly great things are accomplished. A simple little nail made the difference to an entire kingdom. What matters is not the size or the scope of your efforts to be a force for good, but that you do your very best to grow into the type of person you were created to become. This is what will help you clarify your purpose and discover the unique contributions that you and you alone can make in the lives of those around you.

With these key ideas in mind, here are some concrete practices that will help you rise above mediocrity so that you can discover the divine work of love and service that will add vibrancy and meaning to everything you do. As you pursue this path, not only will you help better the lives of others, but you yourself will also be filled with a life-changing sense of purpose—you will discover what it means to live the abundant life.

3 Keys To Rising Above Mediocrity

1. Stand Firm

I remember going on a vacation with my family to visit the giant redwoods in northern California. I marveled in the midst of those giants. Being in their presence made a lifelong impact on me. And yet, those marvels of nature didn't do anything to announce their greatness. They don't have the capacity to advertise themselves to the world or to make their existence known in any other way than to simply be. Just *being themselves* is enough. This is where their power lies; their grandeur is in their pure being.

While on that trip, I documented a few lessons I learned from the redwoods. These ideas are relevant to this chapter and can help us learn what is required to rise above mediocrity in our own lives:

- When a redwood gets injured, it forms burls. These burls then produce offshoots that go directly into the ground to spawn new trees. Even in their adversities, redwoods find ways to grow and become stronger.

- Throughout their entire lives and beyond, redwoods give back to their surroundings. Even after they fall, they continue giving long years of life to ferns and other beautiful plants and animals. In other words, they never really die. They continue to live on through the lives of all the other beings they help provide for. Likewise, our legacy can bless others in ways that extend well beyond the years we have to live on this earth.

- I noted how absolutely straight these trees grow. This is symbolic to me of living what we know, of not deviating from the paths we know to be right, of living a congruent and consistent life. In so doing, we allow ourselves to rise above distractions and temptations that might otherwise stunt our growth. We allow the light to reach us, and our light to reach others.

- A redwood's root system creates a network of huge, wide roots that intertwine with the roots of other redwoods. They support each other. This made me think about how important it is to fill our lives with good mentors, and that we look for ways to give back and mentor others. Truly, we find strength in our connections with others.

- Redwood trees grow a layer of bark that's 6-12 inches thick. This insulates them from extreme temperatures and provides great protection. Having a thick skin is very often necessary to rise above mediocrity. Not everyone will appreciate or respect the life path you've chosen to walk. In fact, some people might openly ridicule your efforts. No matter what others may say or think, it's important to soldier onward for the right reasons. Knowing that your life path is aligned with God will give you the confidence to keep moving forward bravely and with purpose.

There is no question that redwoods have risen to greatness: they are the tallest, largest, longest living trees on earth. Some of them have been alive for several hundred years. Redwoods' ability to not only survive, but to thrive, is a direct result of their deep intertwined roots and their determined growth up toward the sun. Standing firm gives them the strength and protection they need to flourish. When we stand among the redwoods, we learn from their quiet yet powerful dignity. In our own acts of becoming, we too can stand firm, and without the need for fanfare, make a giant difference as we strive to grow into our full potential.

2. Build Your Armor

As I've talked about in earlier chapters, one of the fundamental keys to creating a life of success and happiness is staying true to your Core Values and consistently living what you know to be right. Living this way will empower you to stay true to the course you've charted, and to arrive at your waypoints and destinations with integrity and authenticity.

In order to accomplish all this, however, you need to build fortifications to protect yourself against temptations and distractions that might pull you away from your most important life goals. I like to think of it like building and putting on your spiritual armor. One of the reasons I like this analogy is that it highlights the fact that protecting ourselves against things that might drag us down is not something that just happens. We have to consciously and proactively choose to build and then wear our armor. We have to *act*; we have to assemble our own armor, putting forth the time and effort to search for each piece, creating and customizing it to our unique fit, and making this armor a key part of our daily walk.

One of the best ways to begin building your spiritual armor is to study inspiring sources of truth and wisdom. This could include sacred texts, spiritual teachers, religious leaders, and any other ideas or insights that resonate with you and motivate you to become better. There's nothing more powerful than spending time learning from great mentors and books, working to continuously grow, learn, and develop. This is how you feed your soul and your mind with the truths that will help you in your quest for greatness.

Og Mandino's *The Greatest Salesman in the World* and *The Greatest Salesman in the World, Part II* are two examples of books that contain the type of powerful insights that can help us assemble our armor. Throughout these books, Mandino presents a plan for building and putting on a kind of personal armor that will help us rise above mediocrity. He created what he calls "scrolls" and "vows," which are basically statements designed to help focus our attention on positive, uplifting, and motivating ideas.

He suggests starting out by focusing on the first scroll. After reading it morning, mid-day, and night every day for thirty days straight, it should be firmly planted in your mind and heart. At that point, you're ready to move on to the next scroll. You repeat the process until you've worked through all ten scrolls. For the vows, Mandino suggests a similar process: start with the first vow, read it morning and night for seven days straight, and then move on to the next one. Taken together, Mandino's scrolls and vows are strategies for focusing on and developing positive attitudes, behaviors, and ideas. This is one example of how a person might start crafting their personal armor. Here are Mandino's scrolls and vows:

Ten Scrolls[50]

Scroll 1 - Today I begin a new life: I will form good habits and become their slave.

Scroll 2 - I will greet this day with love in my heart.

Scroll 3 - I will persist until I succeed.

Scroll 4 - I am nature's greatest miracle.

Scroll 5 - I will live this day as if it is my last.

Scroll 6 - Today I will be master of my emotions.

Scroll 7 - I will laugh at the world.

Scroll 8 - Today I will multiply my value a hundredfold.

Scroll 9 - I will act now.

Scroll 10 - I will pray for guidance.

Ten Vows of Success[51]

Vow 1 - Never again will I pity or belittle myself.

Vow 2 - Never again will I greet the dawn without a map.

Vow 3 - Always will I bathe my days in the golden glow of enthusiasm.

Vow 4 - Never again will I be disagreeable to a living soul.

Vow 5 - Always will I seek the seed of triumph in every adversity.

Vow 6 - Never again will I perform any task at less than my best.

Vow 7 - Always will I throw my whole self into the task at hand.

Vow 8 - Never again will I wait and hope for opportunity to embrace me.

Vow 9 - Always will I examine, each night, my deeds of the fading day.

Vow 10 - Always will I maintain contact, through prayer, with my creator.

The armor you fashion as you study and learn from great sources like scriptures, inspiring books, mentors, and your own inner voice will protect and defend the person you are becoming. Keep in mind that even after you've built these types of fortifications in your life, you will still experience challenges and setbacks. But your efforts to protect yourself are what will enable you to remain focused on living a life of purpose, even during the most difficult times. This means that no matter what happens to you or what challenges you encounter you will always be in a position to make a positive impact on the world around you.

3. Be the Unseen Difference

The third key to rising above mediocrity so you can become a positive influence on the world is to become what I call the "unseen difference." To explain what I mean by this, let me share an example from my own life. I first saw Harold Watson as he sat with his large family in church, taking up an entire pew. He was dressed like a gas station worker, his hard-toed, low-top black shoes completing the look. He was clearly in church to worship and didn't care much about making any sort of flashy impression by his appearance. As time went on, we got to know each other and we quickly became good friends.

One day, Harold and his wife invited Ginger and I to his home to socialize and have a few snacks. We were surprised when we pulled up to a long, gated driveway that led to a magnificent 8,000 square foot mansion. As it turned out, my friend owned several gas stations and convenience stores, various other real estate holdings, and was heavily invested in the stock market. The important thing here is not that he had money, it's that he had very obviously never let that money get to his head. He never flaunted his professional or financial success. Instead, he made serving others the focal point of his life.

In the same way that Harold quietly and humbly went about his professional career, never making a big deal about his business success, so too did he quietly and humbly go about serving others. He was a staple of our church community, and he provided incredible amounts of service to all those around him. But, in typical Harold fashion, you would never have known it just by looking at him. He never advertised his efforts to serve and help others. He quietly and humbly focused on building up those around him in whatever ways he could, never caring if anybody knew it or if he ever received any recognition. I eventually adopted Harold as a mentor, and his example of humility—both in terms of his professional success and the way he tried to serve others, including myself—has been hugely influential in my life. He became an unseen difference in my life and in the lives of many others.

When you devote yourself to loving and serving others humbly and sincerely, without fanfare or the need for recognition, you become the unseen difference. Becoming the unseen difference in the lives of those around you is an act of genuine caring without any expectation of receiving honor, acknowledgement, or praise.

When you strive to become the unseen difference, the things you give those you serve will probably not be shared over a podium, from a stage, or in front of cameras. Instead, you'll find yourself sharing sincere moments while relaxing on a porch, sitting around a campfire, or inviting people into your home. Remember my meetings with Jim Ritchie? Those Saturday mornings spent in his Winnebago were some of the most enlightening, formative moments of my entire life. Jim's lessons weren't published online or printed in a journal; they were shared in simple conversations while we relaxed in his RV. Jim didn't receive any big awards for the time he spent mentoring me, but he truly became the unseen difference in my life.

To help you think more concretely about some of the ways you might become the unseen difference, consider some of the ideas shared by author and researcher Tom Rath. In his book *Vital Friends* he outlines eight possible roles people might fill in their relationships with one another:[52]

- **Builder** – A great motivator who pushes others toward the finish line.
- **Champion** – A cheerleader who praises and stands up for their friends.
- **Collaborator** – A person with similar interests who is easy to connect with.
- **Companion** – A friend who's always there for their friends, no matter what.
- **Connector** – A bridge builder who likes to connect their friends and acquaintances with other good people.
- **Energizer** – A fun friend who gives people much-needed boosts of energy.
- **Mind Opener** – A friend who pushes others to expand their horizons

and learn new things.

- **Navigator** – A person who shares good advice and points others in the right direction.

According to Rath, people may play different roles at different times in their lives, or they may find themselves naturally inclined toward a few of them. Either way, it's worth thinking about your strengths and weaknesses, and determining which role or roles you might be best suited to fill. Doing so will help you prepare to become the unseen difference whenever an opportunity arises.

Making A Difference Elevates Your Life

Serving humbly and sincerely, and becoming the unseen difference in the lives of those around you, is the foundation of the abundant life. And in what might seem like a paradox, the act of losing yourself in service actually ends up blessing you in all sorts of amazing ways. If you're focused only on yourself and your personal life, you restrict your existence to a very narrow, severely limited scope. But when you lose yourself in serving and reaching out to others, your life suddenly becomes expansive, even limitless. Your thoughts, concerns, energies, and efforts extend far beyond just yourself, as you begin making a real impact in the lives of those around you.

The real point of working hard to become your best possible self is so that you can make a positive impact on the world. As you strive to follow the life course you've charted with God, look for opportunities to become the unseen difference in the lives of those around you. Remember that the most powerful forms of service are those given through love and genuine care, not for recognition or acclaim. As you devote your life to this type of service, not only will the lives of others be blessed, but your own soul will greatly expand as you find yourself being lifted to new levels of peace, happiness, and a deep sense of purpose.

Application and Relevance

1. Although stretching your limits can be challenging, this is what will help you discover your truest purpose in life. Making a positive impact on the world around you is a key part of this purpose.

2. Remember that small things can make a huge difference.

3. Focus on living the 3 Keys to Rising Above Mediocrity:
   a. **Stand Firm**: Incorporate into your life the lessons of the giant redwood trees.
   b. **Build Your Armor**: Make a conscious effort to protect yourself with the truths and practices you learn from trustworthy and uplifting sources.
   c. **Be The Unseen Difference**: Lose yourself in service to others, and decide not to seek fanfare or recognition for the service you give. Instead, make humility and authenticity your hallmarks of success.

4. Losing yourself in service will allow you to bless others. It will also lift you to new levels of peace, happiness, and purpose.

Notes:

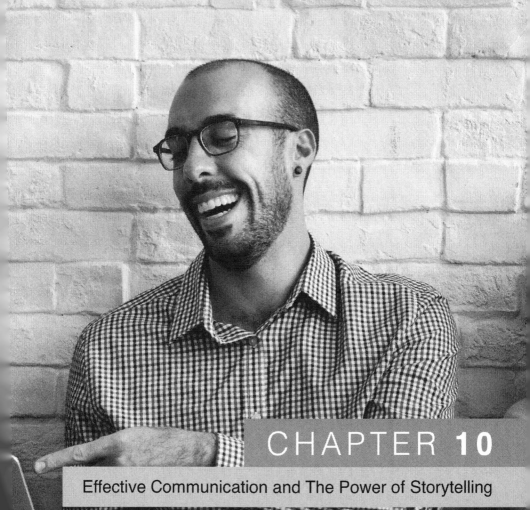

CHAPTER **10**

Effective Communication and The Power of Storytelling

"If the lion does not tell his story, the hunter will."

— African Proverb

We are currently at an interesting point in the history of how humans communicate with one another. We live in a world of sound bites in which a great deal of our communication takes place through shortened words, phrases, and even emoticons. Very often, we communicate using nothing but images. And the connectivity of the digital world means that we're communicating with others *all the time*, whether it's through text messaging, talking on cell phones, on social media, or in online environments like blogs and forums.

The heavy reliance on abbreviated, sound bite-style communication in a world that's also built on non-stop interaction has created a scenario in which communicating is absolutely vital, and yet many people are unable to do so effectively. But this also presents some unique opportunities for setting yourself apart from the crowd. If you can become a master of communication, you will immediately become a valuable addition to any organization or business. Employers, organizers, and professional teams all need people who can help them communicate effectively with clients, potential customers, and their networks. Likewise, if you can communicate effectively with the people in your personal life, you will be able to harness the potential of social media and digital connectivity to help you forge powerful and meaningful connections with people around the world.

As you will discover in this chapter, the key to effective communication is learning to become a powerful storyteller. And that skill is all about knowing how to give people compelling mental images that are linked together to create a logical and persuasive narrative.

The principles of good storytelling are relevant across the board, whether you're talking to somebody face to face, delivering a public address, writing a blog, maintaining a Tumblr, contributing to an online forum, posting to your social media profiles, or adding images to your Instagram account. In each of these environments, powerful storytelling is the best way to communicate clearly and persuasively. Learning this skill will help make you a better leader, contributor, friend, and colleague, and will therefore become a positive influence on the future you create.

The Science Of Storytelling: Why Telling Stories Is So Effective

During the mid-18th century, the British politician and aristocrat John Montagu, the 4th Earl of Sandwich, spent a lot of his free time playing cards. He greatly enjoyed eating snacks while playing, but doing so always made it difficult to hold his cards. Determined to solve this problem, he eventually came up with the idea of putting beef between two slices of toast. This allowed him to eat and play cards at the same time. Eating his newly invented "sandwich," as his new concoction came to be known, Montagu ushered in a new culinary era, as the sandwich quickly became one of the most popular meal creations in the modern world.

The origins of the sandwich don't actually have anything to do with this chapter. But what is interesting about that short paragraph is that you are much more likely to remember where the sandwich came from after reading that story than you would be if I'd just given you raw information like what you would find in an encyclopedia. That's because I taught you about sandwiches by telling you a story. And stories are the easiest way for the human brain to learn and process new information.

For over 27,000 years—since humans first began making cave paintings—telling stories has been one of humanity's most fundamental methods of communication. But why is it so powerful and so effective? What is it about a story that makes such a lasting impression? Why do we feel so deeply engaged when we hear, watch, or read a good story?

The answer has to do with the way our brains are hardwired. If you watch a PowerPoint presentation that contains nothing but boring bullet points of raw information, the only parts of your brain that will be activated are those that deal with language. Scientists call these parts of the brain Broca's area and Wernicke's area. These two regions work together to decode and process language. The PowerPoint presentation that only gives you lines of information will hit these language-processing parts of your brain and that's pretty much it—*nothing else really happens.*

If you want to communicate in a truly engaging and memorable way, you need to activate more parts of the brain. In their amazing book, *Neuromarketing*, authors Patrick Renvoisé and Christophe Morin describe how stories accomplish precisely that.[53] As they explain it, the human brain is composed of three main parts: the "new brain" that controls rational thinking, the "middle brain" that controls emotional processing, and the "old brain" that controls our most basic "fight or flight" instincts, manages our reflex responses, and stores repetitive routines.

Stories activate a wide range of the brain's anatomy, and allow these different parts to start working together. Not only do stories engage the language-processing parts of the brain, they also activate the rational-thinking parts, the emotional-processing parts, and the instinctive, reflexive parts of the brain. Stories activate something called the insula, which is linked to emotion, and which helps us relate to the pain, joy, disgust, or whatever other emotional register the story taps into. Similarly, the sensory cortex goes to work on metaphors and similes as the story brings our senses to life.

While the neurobiological explanation for why stories are so effective is compelling all on its own, it's not the whole picture. Our brains have been designed to look for patterns and connections; it's how we organize the world. A story, if broken down into its simplest form, is a series of cause and effect connections. And that's exactly how we think. Without even realizing it, we think in narratives all day long, whether it's buying groceries, thinking about work, or making plans for what we'll do after work. We make up stories in our heads all the time. It shouldn't be surprising, then, that personal stories and gossip make up 65% of all human conversations.[54] When you tell a story, you give people information in the way that makes the most sense to their brains. No wonder it's so easy to follow along with a good story.

Simply put, stories make the entire brain go to work. The minds of both the person telling the story and the person listening to it light up, and begin to synchronize in very powerful ways. By activating so many parts of the brain at the same time, stories encourage listeners to make connections between the story they're hearing and their own lives, ideas, and experiences. Our brains are always trying to make connections and establish patterns, so when you tell a story you give the brain exactly what it's looking for: a narrative of cause and effect that can help us make sense of our own experiences. The next time you struggle to get your ideas across, try telling a story.

5 Keys To Becoming A Great Storyteller

Key #1: Keep it Simple

It can sometimes be easy to convince ourselves that in order for a story to be compelling and effective it has to be complex and full of intricate details. The truth is, however, that the simpler a story is the more likely it is to stick. Think about the last time you heard someone tell a story that was so long and drawn out that you found yourself begging for it to end. Now compare that to a crisply told story that gets to the point, that doesn't get bogged down in pointless details, and that's captivating the entire time. That's what you're shooting for, so keep your stories simple, succinct, and moving forward. Find the balance of having enough substance to engage your audience, but don't get too carried away trying to weave super complex, difficult to follow tales.

Key #2: Avoid Clichés

Effective storytelling obviously has a lot to do with the actual language you use. Researchers have found that our brains tend to filter out and ignore overused words and phrases.[55] When an expression becomes a cliché, or a word becomes completely commonplace, it fades into the background and doesn't register as something with important meaning.

Clichés are less likely to stick than original words and phrases. But remember to keep it simple. Don't use strange, esoteric, or incomprehensible language; use words and phrases that are clear, accessible, unique, and memorable. The words you use make a difference, so avoid worn out phrases like "once upon a time," and focus instead on building narratives that use a more engaging vocabulary.

Key #3: Incorporate the Elements of a Powerful Story

In his book *Tell to Win* Peter Guber outlines four elements that must be present for a story to be powerful and engaging.[56] When you incorporate these into whatever story you're telling, you can be sure that you'll be communicating effectively.

1. Your story must include **likeable and recognizable characters** that your audience will identify with or empathize with.

2. There must be some sort of **drama**, some **uncertainty**, or some **anticipation** involved. Something out of the ordinary needs to happen to create tension and uncertainty about the outcome of the story. You want your audience to wonder what will happen next and be concerned with how things will turn out in the end.

3. Your story needs a "Eureka moment" in which the **central character breaks through and does something great.** Your story has to deliver its payload.

4. You need something that will help your listeners realize that the story you're telling actually has relevance to their own lives. As the listener **makes an emotional connection** with the story, they will suddenly realize that their life somehow shares some of the same dynamics as the narrative they're listening to. A meaningful story always tells listeners what's in it for them, and will give them something they can use as they move forward with their lives.

To show you how these elements play out in an actual narrative, here's a true story that Jim Ritchie often tells when he teaches (the names of those involved have been changed to protect their privacy):

Clyde Belfry and his brother Frank grew up in the hills of Uganda, in central Africa. The two brothers, about ten and eleven at the time, would arise early in the morning and trek their way into the foothills, protecting their growing goat herd and making sure they had food and water. This type of sustainable living (raising goats) is a key way to get ahead in Uganda; as the goat herd grows, so do the family's opportunities. Clyde and Frank assumed they'd spend the rest of their days performing these worthwhile labors until a disaster unexpectedly struck.

A deadly disease originating in Europe invaded Uganda, and quickly devastated the country's goats. Nearly every goat in Uganda died from the disease, including all of the Belfry family's small herd. The disease left the family without any chance of financial success; they were destitute and desperate.

In the middle of this incredible setback, Clyde decided to strike out on his own as a young teenager and see what was on the other side of the mountain. With his meager belongings strapped to his back, he walked the many miles to the "big city," where he somehow got himself enrolled in a school and worked hard to obtain a high school diploma. He did so well academically that he was awarded a scholarship to attend a university, which in turn paved the way for him to eventually enroll at Oxford University in England.

Graduating from Oxford with honors, he returned to a good paying job with the Ugandan government, which made him a man of influence and privilege. He married and began raising a family. His son Winston grew up under a very different set of circumstances than Clyde had, and after finishing high school, he was admitted to the University of Washington, where he received a degree and landed a prominent job in Washington D.C.

Upon reflection of his and his family's good fortunes, Clyde thought back to the days of his youth, and wondered aloud "What if the goats had not died?"

Let's break down this story by highlighting how each of the four elements of a powerful story are present:

1. **Likeable and recognizable characters.** Who doesn't love a family of goat herders working hard to make an honest living? Who can't relate to or empathize with this family, working together to sustain life? This story is full of characters that it's easy to root for.

2. **Drama, uncertainty, or anticipation.** The disease that killed the family's goats created the tension and uncertainty around which the entire story revolves.

3. **Breakthrough moment when main character does something great.** The teenage boy venturing out from his home, going over the mountains to attend school and make his own mark is the story's breakthrough moment.

4. **Emotional connection.** Readers and listeners can easily relate to the way Clyde's act of courage dramatically altered his family's fortunes. The reader can reflect on her own life and identify a challenge that's kind of like her own "dead goat story." After hearing how Clyde

turned his trial into a blessing, listeners gain new insights into their own life difficulties and can find motivation to confront them.

Depending on the context in which a story is told, adding pictures and other images can be an incredible way to further enhance the impact of the narrative. In those cases, the same principles of good storytelling and effective communication should be used to help you tell a story with images. Be intentional about the images you choose to display and the way in which you present them to your audience. Be sure that you're visually narrating a tale that will speak to your audience's need for order, identification, and learning.

Key #4: Follow the Three E's

The next time you have to deliver some sort of presentation or give a speech, consider leading with a story. Personal stories can be especially effective ways to grab your listeners' attention and get them to engage with what you're saying. In addition to what we've covered already, focus on building your story or presentation around the "Three E's of Effective Communication:"

Energize: Tell stories about people who overcame tough challenges and came out winners. Stories of perseverance are compelling and inspiring, and can give your words a sense of positive energy. Craft stories and messages that:

- Motivate and inspire
- Build courage
- Help others find passion in their lives

Educate: The stories you tell should give something of value to your audience. In your stories try to:

- Teach important lessons
- Provide coaching or relevant feedback
- Show good problem-solving in action

Empower: When you empower someone, you give that person the knowledge and tools they need to succeed. In your efforts to communicate, teach, and tell stories, invite people to use the concepts you're sharing with them to take some sort of action that will lead them toward success. In particular, try to:

- Encourage people to follow their instincts
- Give people permission to excel
- Invite the audience to take the reins and control their own destiny

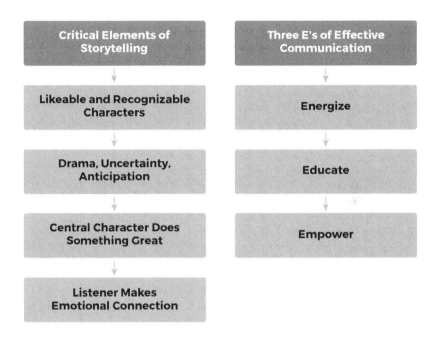

Key #5: Prepare and Practice

Although really good storytellers often look like they're just spontaneously spinning a good tale, trust me, the ease with which they communicate doesn't just come out of the blue; it's the outcome of dedicated preparation and practice.

The preparation that's necessary to become a great storyteller starts with keeping an eye and an ear open for good stories. The first and most important source of stories worth telling is your own life. Look for ways you might be able to use personal experiences to teach important principles or to connect with others.

You should also pay attention for good stories you hear from others. Great stories are often told, retold, and used in a variety of different settings. I recommend creating a system for collecting and saving the great stories you hear from others. Try making a folder on your computer or mobile device into which you can add great stories you find. When you find something good online, save the page and drop it into your folder. If you hear a good story, type it out and then add the document to the folder. Once you've got a good collection going, you can start organizing your stories by topic, characters, key lessons, or anything else that makes sense to you. This will make it easy to find the right story whenever you need it.

Once you've got stories to tell, you need to practice telling them. Mark Twain once said, "It usually takes me more than three weeks to prepare a good impromptu speech."[57] Practice really does make perfect, and that holds true when it comes to your ability to communicate effectively.

I have a good friend who is perhaps the world's best presenter; I really mean it, he is legendary. He practices speaking in front of a mirror all the time. He rehearses over and over again, focusing on all aspects of his delivery. He practices his facial expressions, his gestures, the timing of powerful lines, where he'll add a little well-placed humor, and the lessons he's trying to get across. He didn't become the best in the world by just winging it, he did so through dedicated preparation and practice.

How To Tell If You're Communicating Effectively

One of the best advocates for the power of storytelling as an effective mode of communication is Paul Smith. In his book *Lead With A Story*, he outlines some things you can look for that will help you know if you're doing a good job of using stories to become a great communicator. [58]

In particular, Smith makes connections between becoming a good leader and the art of storytelling. For him, the two are intertwined in all sorts of important ways. Smith suggests that as you begin honing your storytelling and communicating skills you look for the following outcomes, trends, and patterns:

- Are your leadership skills starting to improve? The more you focus on being a good storyteller, the more people will begin listening to your stories, and the better they'll grasp what you want them to do or understand. This, in turn, will allow you and the people you're communicating with to work more collaboratively and productively.

- Are you starting to hear your own stories being told back to you, sometimes by people you may not even know? Great stories are viral. They will crop up all over the place again and again. If people remember the stories you tell and the messages you communicate, don't be surprised to see that story take on a life of its own. When you hear some version of your story echoed back by other people in other contexts, you know you're succeeding in your quest to become an effective storyteller.

- Are you instinctively turning to storytelling? The better you become at using stories to help you communicate, the more your first instinct will be to find a good story to tell whenever you find yourself in a situation where effective communication is needed. This will happen naturally as you realize firsthand that stories are the best way to move people and make things happen.

Most of us are not natural storytellers. But after reading this chapter, hopefully you're starting to buy into the idea that telling stories is a true key to success—buying into it at least enough to give it a shot. We can all become effective communicators in all spheres of life if we diligently prepare and practice. Learning the art of storytelling truly can help you shape and create your future. It's worth the effort and will most definitely add color and vibrancy to your life and to the lives of those around you.

Application and Relevance

1. To become an effective communicator you need to learn the art of storytelling.

2. Stories are such a powerful way to communicate because they activate the entire brain, provide a way for people to make connections between themselves and others, and appeal to the brain's natural tendency to construct narratives.

3. Focus on The 5 Keys to Becoming an Effective Storyteller:
    I.   Keep It Simple
    II. Avoid Clichés
    III. Incorporate the Elements of a Powerful Story:
         a. Likable and recognizable characters
         b. Drama, uncertainty, or anticipation
         c. Central character does something great
         d. Emotional connection

    IV. Follow the Three E's:
         a. Energize
         b. Educate
         c. Empower

    V.   Prepare and Practice

4. Decide to hone the art of storytelling, as it is the secret sauce to the most effective communication.

Notes:

CHAPTER **11**

Giving Back

"I knew a man, they thought him mad, the more he gave, the more he had."

— Anonymous

The Most Important Part Of The Formula

You'll remember from Chapter 5 that the last step in The Formula is "Give Back." This concept is so important that we've devoted an entire chapter to it. Jim Ritchie, one of the founders of Launching Leaders, pieced together The Formula through a combination of advice he received from mentors, ideas he picked up in great books, and his own experiences as a successful entrepreneur and devoted religious leader. Whenever he explains The Formula to someone, Jim stresses that the true indicator of how well a person is living The Formula is how much they've centered their life on giving back to others, whether it's through giving money, time, talents, teaching, mentoring, or in any other way. Giving back is the key to the entire thing. Here's how Jim explains it:

At the pinnacle of success in my career, I went to visit one of my life mentors, a man named David Haight. This was the same man who 14 years earlier had first introduced me to The Formula. I sat in his office and asked him if I was on the right track, as I was then getting ready to retire so I could focus on becoming a volunteer teacher. I wanted to teach the world the same principles of success that had such a profound effect on my life, and I wanted to make this knowledge available to everyone for free.

David said, "Do you really know The Formula?"

I said, "Yes, I think I do."

Then he said, "Think about it. If you get up early, work hard, get your education, discover your passion, and make your mark in the world through this passion, it's almost impossible to not be successful. It's simply the result of living The Formula."

"But if you miss the most important step," he continued, "the success you seek will, in the end, destroy you with the pride and arrogance that comes with the riches of the world. If, however, you really got The Formula well, you will understand that if you live it for the right reasons—which are to help OTHER people be successful and to be a mentor to them and to give back what you have—then it will keep you humble enough that you will not be destroyed by your own success."

Giving back is how you truly fill your life with meaning and purpose. It's how you keep your life aligned with the divine and the spiritual every day so that you can become the person you're meant to become, and so that you can discover the purpose for which you were made.

Giving Back As Part Of Your Daily Walk

Our children have become fans of TV cooking shows, and I've been drawn in a few times to watch the way different chefs prepare and present their food. Certainly everyone can relate to the experience of enjoying a truly great meal. Sometimes just the memory of an amazing meal can make your mouth start to water. And although watching a person prepare food on TV can be fun and interesting, there's no substitute for actually being able to see, smell, and taste the meal itself. The same is true of giving back. The power, love, and joy created through the process of giving are most fully felt in the actual, lived experience of helping another person.

This seems to be a concept that the Millennial generation already understands. That's why so many Millennials place high value on giving back whenever they can, in whatever ways they can, and as often as they can. They don't want to wait until later in life to start giving back. Millennials seem to understand just how powerful giving is, and they want to make it a central part of their lives *right now*, in the present. They want their journey through life to be filled with actually *tasting* and *participating* in the act of giving, not just hearing about it or watching others do it.

In previous generations, there was an attitude that giving back came only *after* a person had gained financial self-reliance, which then made it possible for them to give through some large project or donation. But it seems as if Millennials are turning that assumption on its head. I love the way Millennials approach giving back as something that should happen all the time throughout the journey of life rather than only at the end, after a person has already achieved financial security (see Chapter 8). Of course, financial well-being will open up all sorts of opportunities to give back in really powerful ways, but you shouldn't wait to start giving back until you achieve financial security. Just as you need food and water on an almost daily basis to survive, giving back should become a key component of your daily life; think of it as part of a continuous process rather than a single big event. To help you make giving back an important part of your daily walk, here are some key concepts to keep in mind.

Keys To Giving Back

Key #1: Focus On Making Connections

We can carry the cooking show analogy a bit further. In the same way that there's no real substitute for the experience of actually eating a meal, there's no real substitute for giving back and helping others in a direct, face to face way. This isn't to say that making a money donation to people or organizations you won't ever actually meet is somehow bad or wrong. Instead, what I'm trying to say is that one of the most incredible things about giving back is that it helps create new connections and foster new relationships, all built on a foundation of love. Anytime you're able to serve somebody in a more direct way, those connections can become stronger, more real, and more meaningful.

In addition, giving back in a direct, personal way can sometimes require that you give more of yourself. There is a big difference between writing a check for a well to be dug in central Africa and helping to dig the hole yourself. There is a difference between ordering flowers for a friend in the hospital and taking the time to go visit them in person. Again, I'm not saying there's anything wrong with donating money to a well-digging campaign or ordering flowers for a friend; in fact those are both very good things. But when you give to others in direct, personal ways, you're giving more of your self—not only your money, but your time, energy, and effort as well—and as a result, the connections you'll make with those you serve will be deeper and more meaningful.

There's one more type of connection that giving back helps facilitate, and that's your personal connection with the divine. Since none of us would exist without the presence of some higher power, we are all the recipients of the greatest gift of all: life itself. It is this divine, higher power that has given us everything we have and are, so when we focus on giving back and serving others, we are also fostering a connection to that divine force. In a very real sense, we enter into the divine project of giving and serving. Ultimately, then, giving back allows us to strengthen connections and grow in some truly remarkable ways.

Key #2: Cultivate A Giving Heart

When it comes to the way we serve and give back to others, the thing that matters most is our intent. If we give back as a self-serving way to showcase our good deeds and prosperity, we're not truly giving. But if we give back with the right attitude and intent, we are serving in a Godly way, in a way that will help us become something greater and that will enable us to cultivate a giving heart. When our hearts are turned from profit to people, regardless if it makes financial sense or not, then our giving becomes authentic. Something magical happens when we turn our hearts toward the needs of others and our focus starts to turn outward rather than inward.

Personal gain or recognition should never be part of our efforts to give back. However, and not coincidentally, the process of giving back and serving others benefits both the giver and the receiver. Acts of authentic service and love that come from a giving heart bless everyone involved, as the person giving the service and the person receiving the service both feel the love of God at work. Together, they both draw closer to God.

Sincere service and authentic giving—based on a genuine desire to help others and not a wish for recognition or praise—will create powerful bonds with the people around you and with the divine. Of course, it's impossible to have a pure heart 100% of the time. But even if you sense imperfect motives and feelings, don't let that keep you from giving and serving. As you offer up your imperfections to the Lord and choose to do the right thing, even though your heart may not be fully in it, you allow your heart to be changed. As you continue making the right decisions and attempt to work out your impurities, you will gradually begin developing a sincere and giving heart.

Key #3: Match Your Giving To Your Passion

There are so many possible ways to give back. Before you assume that donating money is the only way to give, you should consider the full range of what you're capable of contributing to those around you. And as with everything else, you should use the Cycle of Spiritual Guidance to help you discover the ways you're best fit to serve.

Since there are literally an infinite number of ways to give back, you need to focus on matching your efforts to give back with your natural passions and gifts. The way you live out the passions within you says a lot about who you really are. In Chapter 1's discussion of the Cycle of Spiritual Guidance, you learned how important it is to act on spiritual impressions right away. As you try to find the most effective and meaningful way to give back to others, try to come up with creative ways to put your natural passions and skills to work, and pay attention to the inspiration of your inner voice. For example, somebody who's passionate about teaching could put their passion to work by volunteering at an after school mentoring program. Somebody who loves sports might volunteer to be a coach. Another person who loves writing could teach writing workshops at a jail. And a business-minded person might donate their expertise to up and coming entrepreneurs or to people trying to start a business in economically disadvantaged places. There really are limitless ways to serve. The trick is to identify your passions and skills, and then use the guidance of your inner voice to find ways to use your gifts that will make somebody else's life a little bit better.

Finding one's passion and then using it as a way to give back is exactly what Launching Leaders Worldwide graduate Matthew is doing in Ghana. After learning about the good work Matthew is doing, Launching Leaders Worldwide decided to partner with him in his efforts to give back. This is how Matthew describes his efforts to match his giving to his passion:

I am a survivor and refugee from the civil war in Liberia. I fled for my life on a small fishing boat, not even knowing where it was going. For four days without food, I survived on rainwater until the boat landed in Ghana.

As a boy growing up I remembered my late father—who died during the civil war in Liberia—tell me, "Matthew, always learn to share or give because you never know when you will have enough." I did experience poverty growing up; it was difficult for me as a boy to share with my friends the little I had to eat for the day, but I always remembered my father's teaching.

I got out of the refugee camps in Ghana as a part-time teacher. I know what hunger is because I have experienced it. I know what it feels like not to be in school. I know what it means to be sacked from school due to non-payment of school fees. I know what it means to go to school with bare feet on the ground. I know what it feels like to go to school without a pencil, or notebooks or a uniform; I passed through it all. These things inspired me to help others that are less fortunate than me. I don't want any children to go through what I went through in getting an education all because of lack, often caused by the death of their parents. I want them to have the chance to live a better life.

By no coincidence I met the founders of Launching Leaders through books they had written. I adopted them as mentors, and they also adopted me in helping to establish Launching Leaders in Ghana, as well as the fund I started, Matthew's Fund. I find and help rescue young children and their single mothers from the refugee camps and enroll them in schools. The young adults and single mothers are taught the principles of Launching Leaders. Together, through Matthew's Fund and Launching Leaders, we hope to change generations.

I believe God answered my prayers in bringing us together.[59]

Matthew's passion for helping others avoid some of the trials he went through, as well as his passion for learning, led him to create a program that moves young people out of refugee camps and into places where they can receive an education. His work is an effort to live what Matthew says is one of his favorite quotes from Nelson Mandela: "Education is the most powerful weapon which you can use to change the world."[60]

Giving back doesn't have to be groundbreaking, grandiose, or monumental. If you've developed a giving heart, and you're striving to use your innate skills and passions for the benefit of others, your efforts to give back will certainly make a difference.

The Fundamentals Of Selflessness

When you make giving back a regular part of who you are and how you live your daily walk, you will find yourself becoming less self-centered and more selfless. The move from self-centeredness to selflessness is a truly life-changing transformation. Because it's such an important undertaking, Launching Leaders Worldwide has developed a set of benchmarks that will help you gauge how well you're doing in this pursuit. Use this as a tool to check in with yourself and to identify those places that need improving.

The Fundamentals Of Selflessness

1. **Value:** Serving others and giving back has value that cannot be measured in worldly terms.

   Giving is not an investment with an anticipated rate of return. In fact, the value of the gift is usually not monetary. If you give without any anticipation of a return favor or act of kindness, you are living the fundamental of value. If you give from the heart, the value of your gift and your service is priceless.

2. **Stewardship:** Being a good steward means you carefully and responsibly take care of something that's been entrusted to your care. Recognizing the source of your blessings will help you be a good steward of whatever you've been blessed with.

   We ought to look upon the gifts or means we've been blessed with as a valuable treasure that is expected to be shared with others. If we strive to bless others as we are blessed, our service then becomes a source of peace that benefits more lives than just our own. This is what it means to live the fundamental of stewardship.

3. **Abundance:** Your understanding of abundance will determine how readily you place other people's needs and interests first.

   I remember one of my grandchildren pulling a sucker out of his mouth and offering me a lick. Although I declined the offer, since I knew how precious that sucker was to him, I was touched by his genuine act of kindness. The fact that he was interested in sharing something with me that was dear to him was profound, I thought, for a two year old. If we are generous in our efforts to put the interests of others first, even if it requires sacrifice, we are living the fundamental of abundance.

4. **Authenticity:** The most valuable gift you have to offer is your real self.

   The idea of authenticity centers around understanding your true identity and of knowing that your efforts to serve and give back can be a powerful tool for good in the world. In order for this to happen, however, your heart must be aligned with God. When you give back with a sincere heart, with pure intentions, and as an effort to develop your true identity as a spiritual person of worth, you are living the fundamental of authenticity.

5. **Receptivity:** One of the most overlooked aspects of giving back is the need to stay open to *receiving* service just as much as you give it. This will allow you to create bonds of love that are truly cooperative and that flow in both directions.

   If you are a natural giver, receiving can sometimes be very difficult. And yet, to not receive with gratitude is to diminish the power of giving back, and is to deny somebody else the ability to make giving back part of their daily walk. With this understanding, I should have accepted a lick from my grandchild's sucker!

I remember when a very difficult thing happened to me and my wife Ginger. A good friend heard the bad news and immediately drove over to our house to say they loved us and to give us big hugs. I was so grateful for that simple act of kindness. Ginger and I didn't try to hide or diminish the fact that we were hurting; we accepted our friend's love and care with gratitude and the three of us shared a moving moment of love and friendship. When we open our hearts to receiving with gratitude we are living the fundamental of receptivity.

In Conclusion

Your desires and efforts to give back might not be considered "grandiose," but as long as they enrich somebody's life they are worthy and priceless. Instead of trying to measure the size of your attempts to give, you should realize that it all makes a difference. The lyrics of a children's song I sang at church as a young boy capture this thought perfectly:

"Give," said the little stream,
"Give oh give! Give oh give!"
"Give," said the little stream,
As it hurried down the hill.
"I'm small, I know, but wherever I go
The fields grow greener still."

Singing, singing all the day
"Give away, oh, give away."
Singing, singing all the day,
"Give oh give away."[61]

The woman who wrote the lyrics to this song, Fanny Crosby, became blind at six weeks of age due to medical malpractice. And yet, what might seem like a challenge prepared her to give back to the world by writing more than 8,000 inspiring hymns and songs of praise. The tragedy that took away her eyesight did not deter her passion or her ability to discover the greater purpose of her life. She said this about her blindness: "It seemed intended by the blessed providence of God that I should be blind all my life, and I thank him for the dispensation. If perfect earthly sight were offered me tomorrow I would not accept it. I might not have sung hymns to the praise of God if I had been distracted by the beautiful and interesting things about me."[62]

Crosby made giving back a part of her daily walk by working with whatever skills, passions, and opportunities her life presented her with. As she worked to pursue her gifts, and as she found ways to use those gifts to benefit others, she developed her true identity.

Your path may be to visit the sick and read them stories. It may be to assist local charities in their good causes. It may be to stand firm in your Core Values in the face of a wavering world. It may be to give back to your family or to be there for your friends and for those around you who might need a helping hand, a listening ear, or a shoulder to cry on. Whatever it is, pursue it with passion. As you make giving back a key part of your daily walk your world will change from black and white to living color in hi-definition; it will be indescribably beautiful.

Application and Relevance

1. Remember that giving back is the ultimate point of The Formula. It's what makes The Formula a unique self-help strategy and it's what allows you to imbue your pursuit of success with a deep sense of spirituality and meaning.

2. Don't put off service until you think you're "more prepared;" start giving back and serving those around you right now through small, simple, everyday acts of service.

3. Make giving back a part of your daily walk by remembering these three keys:
   a. Focus on making connections
   b. Cultivate a giving heart
   c. Match your giving to your passion

4. Giving back may take many shapes and forms. To discover how you can give back, follow your passions and skills, figure out how to use them to benefit others, and pay attention to the guidance of your inner voice.

5. Make authenticity and humility the hallmarks of your efforts to give back.

Notes:

_____

_____

_____

_____

_____

_____

_____

_____

_____

_____

_____

_____

_____

_____

_____

_____

_____

_____

_____

_____

CHAPTER 12

Onward!

"A life lived with integrity—even if it lacks the trappings of fame and fortune—is a
shining star in whose light others may follow in the years to come."

— Denis Waitley[63]

What an amazing and truly life-changing journey we've been on together throughout this book. Even before you first began turning the pages of *Launching Leaders*, you were already a person of infinite worth and value. Your life has always been filled with meaning and purpose. This book is intended to help you discover deeper levels of worth, value, meaning, and purpose that you may not have even known could be yours. It is intended to help you access a new depth of completeness, and to help you become more than you already are. Ultimately, it is intended to help you reach new heights by imbuing *all* aspects of your life with a deep sense of spiritual vitality and authenticity.

This book hinges on the fundamental belief that each and every one of us are spiritual beings of infinite worth and limitless potential. Recognizing these truths and making them the central components of your identity are the keys to building a life of lasting happiness and success. That's exactly why this book has focused on teaching you the concepts and skills that will enable you to bring all aspects of who you are and how you live into alignment with God, so that your daily walk—including everything from work to school to hanging out with friends to studying to carving out alone time for yourself and everything in between—will be a spiritually empowered one. Not only will this allow you to become everything you were created to be, but it will also fill your life with a sense of peace, purpose, and happiness that cannot be found in any other way.

So now that you've read *Launching Leaders*, how will you actually incorporate what you've learned into your daily life? How will you remember and practice these principles? How will you make them part of who you are and how you live? Your life is busy, and sometimes it will feel like you're being pulled in every direction except the one you're trying to travel. When this happens, how will you bring your life back onto the course you've charted and get yourself pointed once again toward your waypoints and your destinations?

Whatever challenges you may encounter and whatever your past may have been, the future lays ahead. Now is the time to put into practice all the things you've learned and to use the light of these principles to create the life you most desire. Now is the time to move *onward* toward greatness and toward the victories of your life.

Don't Look Back

I've already mentioned a couple times my involvement with farming. I love farming, and I think there are so many powerful lessons it can teach us. One of those lessons is that empowering ourselves isn't something that just happens magically all by itself; it requires a conscious decision to learn correct principles and then a dedicated pattern of actually doing and living them. You can't just expect your crops to grow all on their own. Becoming a successful farmer requires a conscious and committed effort to cultivate healthy soil, sow the seeds, nourish the plants, and eventually, to harvest and store the fruit.

To take this farming analogy a bit further, imagine a farmer during the early 1800s. Without the help of motorized equipment like we have today, this farmer is probably a strong man with sinewy arms and a firm step, striving to guide the blade of the plow straight and true as he attempts to subdue the wilderness. The horse pulling the plow is digging deep for traction and gasping for breath. The ground seems to be battling the blade, but the man's focus is intent as he looks toward the furrow to be cut. Hour after hour, until the earth gives way, he never looks back except to see that the row is straight and his progress true.

Of all the work of the field, plowing is the heaviest labor. That's because when a farmer plows, he's disturbing what's already settled into place, he's breaking apart the conventional, overturning the status quo, literally creating a new future. What once was an unproductive stretch of land, after being plowed and planted, will eventually become a field capable of sustaining life. And all of this requires toil and sweat—it demands hard work.

With that image in mind, I'd like you to think about all the ideas you've encountered in this book as seeds of success. Through the process of reading *Launching Leaders*, you've already started plowing rows in which these seeds can be planted. So far, it may have been a bit of a battle. You may have experienced opposition to your efforts to change, to implement new principles of faith into your life, to rise above, and to blaze a path of excellence. But simply by the fact that you've made it this far in the book, you've already succeeded in carving out enough space for some of these seeds to be planted. You've put your hand to the plow, and you've begun planting the seeds of success.

What is required now is to keep your hand on the plow without turning back. You need to keep doing the work that you've started by reading this book; you need to continue plowing and planting. As a farmer, I can tell you that cultivating greatness is a process of continual work. After the hard labor of preparing the fields and planting the seeds comes the hard work of nurturing your young plants, and eventually, of harvesting the fruits of your efforts. Although it's a difficult process, there is nothing better and more fulfilling than watching your hard work create something truly life-giving and life-sustaining. This is where the farmer finds his deepest sense of purpose and meaning.

Now that you've got your seeds and have started plowing, you will soon see the principles you've planted start to sprout and begin to grow. These sprouts will require nourishment and care to grow into strong plants with deep roots. But the effort required to give them the attention they need will be rewarding in and of itself, as you watch the miraculous process of growth and transformation unfold in your life. And in the end, this continuous effort is what will eventually yield a truly abundant harvest. Here are some things to focus on as you begin the work of nurturing the seeds of success.

Nurturing The Seeds Of Success

1. Keep a Journal

Adversity is a natural and unavoidable part of life, and one of the keys to making it through difficult and challenging times is to cling to what you know to be right and true. But in the heat of the battle and in the moment of adversity, how will you *remember* the principles you've learned? Keeping a journal is a powerful way to keep yourself focused on what matters most. Regularly writing in your journal will help you steer your life toward the waypoints you've established and will keep your trajectory centered on the course you've charted.

At the end of a Launching Leaders session, we asked several graduates how they were going to remember the all the principles they'd learned. One response, from a 20-something named Elle, really stood out:

"Shortly after I started taking the Launching Leaders courses, I began to keep a journal. I divided it into three parts: 1) Areas I believe I'm excelling in, 2) Areas

I need to improve, and 3) Service to others.

I found that after a few weeks, the area of service was blank; really very little was in my life surrounding service. Keeping a journal was how this became evident to me. I was then able to focus on what mattered most to me and change an aspect of my life that I was very passionate about, but which I had not identified as lacking until I kept a journal." [64]

There are a few important points in what Elle said that are worth thinking more about. First, she developed an approach to journaling that worked for her and that was specifically tailored to her personal goals, interests, and needs. Second, she stuck with it; she made journaling a regular part of her life. And third, she used her journaling as a way of both documenting her life and checking in with herself. Her journal became a tool enabling her to make real progress toward her most important life goals.

Keeping a journal will help you remember the principles you've learned in *Launching Leaders* and will help you in your quest to become the person you want to be. Journaling allows you to reflect on how far you've come and contemplate the path ahead. It can help you work through challenges, as well as recognize all the good things in your life. In doing all this, it will also help you create a life of happiness, satisfaction, and fulfillment right now, in the present.

2. Connect with the Spiritual

I was raised in a small town in northern Wyoming that was named after my great-grandfather, Byron Sessions. During the 1800s, he helped lead a group of settlers into the Big Horn Basin. In the process of taming the land, his company was contracted by the U.S. government to build a canal that would bring water to the entire region.

This was a time of hand shovels, horse-drawn equipment, and small explosives. Byron and the rest of the company worked hard, digging away, until they ran right into a massive boulder. They needed to excavate this boulder to continue on, but it was so big they couldn't dig down deep enough to pull it out of the ground. They couldn't go around it because of the topography of the land. Nobody knew how they were going to solve this dilemma and complete the canal, so Byron ordered his team out of the hole.

Byron was a man of faith who believed he could connect with the Lord through prayer. Early the next morning, before any other workers arrived, he knelt beside the rock and prayed mightily for some way to get through the huge boulder. Later that day, he had a strong spiritual impression that a way would be opened up, although it still seemed completely hopeless. Acting on faith, he told his workers that the problem with the rock would be resolved by "this time tomorrow." One man looked at his watch; it was 4:00p.m.

The next afternoon, he ordered the workers out of the hole and told everyone to get away from the boulder. They quickly obeyed orders. Five minutes had not passed when the rock suddenly split from top to bottom, the larger half rolling into the hole where the men had been working. The man from the day before again looked at his watch. "Five minutes to four," he exclaimed.

Today, the canal quietly rolls between the two halves of what is now known as "Prayer Rock." It is a state landmark, a testament to what can be accomplished when we combine hard work, prayer, and faith.

Because of my family connection to this story, it has special meaning to me. I commissioned a well-known artist named Glen Hopkinson to create a painting of the event. The young children he painted are there to represent my own grandchildren. Now, when I show them this painting and tell them this story, I can talk to them about the power of prayer and the importance of connecting with the spiritual side of life.

Although most of us will probably never have an experience as dramatic as Byron's, connecting with and tapping into spiritual power is something that will bless all of our lives. For Byron, praying is what allowed him to access spiritual power. Depending on your personal beliefs and practices, it might be meditating, studying scripture, reciting sacred words, or simply taking time to enjoy the beauty of nature. Whatever it is that lets you focus on the spiritual side of things and connect with the divine, do it. Cultivate your relationship with the sacred, your personal link to some higher power. As you continue on your life journey, tap into the power of spirituality and let it feed the seeds of success you've already started to plant.

3. Become the Captain of Your Soul

The British poet William Earnest Henley once wrote an inspiring poem about the power of maintaining hope and determination in the face of even the toughest odds. He titled his poem "Invictus," which is a Latin word meaning "unconquerable." This poem offers some ideas and insights that perfectly parallel many of the overall themes of *Launching Leaders*. I suggest that you read and re-read this poem—maybe even memorize it—so that it can inspire you and give you motivation to press on in the course you've charted, to stay true to your Core Values, to keep your life aligned with God, to take charge of your life, and, as Henley puts it, to become the captain of your soul.

Invictus

Out of the night that covers me,
Black as the Pit from pole to pole,
I thank whatever gods may be
For my unconquerable soul.

In the fell clutch of circumstance
I have not winced nor cried aloud.
Under the bludgeonings of chance
My head is bloody, but unbowed.

Beyond this place of wrath and tears
Looms but the Horror of the shade,
And yet the menace of the years
Finds, and shall find, me unafraid.

It matters not how strait the gate,
How charged with punishments the scroll.
I am the master of my fate:
I am the captain of my soul.[65]

A Final Question

A few years ago, I served as a volunteer pastor for a church congregation made up almost entirely of Millennials. Throughout my time with them, I met with members of the congregation as often as I could to have one-on-one talks with them about their life journeys. The question I always asked them was:

How will the world be different because you lived?

I now ask you the same thing. As you ponder that question, I hope you can feel the confidence and respect I have for you. I hope you can see the vision I have for your happiness, peace, and success, and most importantly, I hope you can sense your own limitless potential for greatness and joy.

I hope this book has given you insights, ideas, and concrete practices that will enable you to imbue your everyday life with a deep sense of spirituality, authenticity, and meaning. I invite you to pay it forward by sharing what you've learned with others. Most of all, I wish you an amazing, spirit-filled, and rewarding life—and somehow in my heart, I know you are well on your way!

God bless you as you Create Your Future!

Application and Relevance

1. Now that you've finished reading this book, it's time to keep your hand on the plow, plant the seeds of success, and nurture those seeds so they can grow into strong plants with deep roots.

2. As you plant the seeds of success in your life, nourish and protect them by keeping a journal, tapping into spiritual power, and working to become the captain of your soul.

3. Find joy in both the process of cultivating greatness and in the eventual harvest.

4. Ask yourself how the world will be different because you lived.

5. Now that you're on the path to happiness, purpose, and success it's time to keep going. It's time to move ONWARD!

Notes:

_____

_____

_____

_____

_____

_____

_____

_____

_____

_____

_____

_____

_____

_____

_____

_____

_____

_____

_____

_____

_____

NOTES

1   Fulghum, Robert, Third Wish (Bellevue, Washington: becker&mayer! Books, 2009).

2   McKeown, Greg, Essentialism: The Disciplined Pursuit of Less (New York: Crown Business, 2014), 15.

3   Broughton, Reni. "Untitled poem." Poem performed at National New Zealand Young Single Adults Conference Variety Show, February 7, 2015. Used with permission.

4   McGill, Bryant H. "Bryant H. McGill Quotes." Inspirational Quotes, Words, Sayings. Accessed May 6, 2016. http://www.inspirationalstories.com/quotes/t/bryant-h-mcgill/.

5   Quoted in: Daft, Richard L., The Executive and the Elephant: A Leader's Guide for Building Inner Excellence (San Francisco: Jossey-Bass, 2010), 246.

6   Exodus 3:5, New Living Translation. Emphasis added.

7   Quoted in: Toastmaster (June 2015), 8. Accessed June 9, 2016. https://www.toastmasters.org/~/media/EB1D553A608043BA91AD5347F1FF178D.ashx

8   National Honey Board. "Honey Trivia." National Honey Board. Accessed May 6, 2016. http://www.honey.com/newsroom/press-kits/honey-trivia.

9   Ibid.

10 Maxwell, Neal A. "The Stern but Sweet Seventh Commandment." New Era (June 1979). Accessed May 17, 2016. https://www.lds.org/new-era/1979/06/the-stern-but-sweet-seventh-commandment?lang=eng.

11 Wadhwa, Vivek. "Don't Confuse Investors with Mentors." The Wall Street Journal (May 20, 2013). Accessed April 22, 2016. http://blogs.

wsj.com/accelerators/2013/05/20/vivek-wadhwa-dont-confuse-investors-with-mentors/.

12 Kimmelman, Michael. "ART REVIEW; El Greco, Bearer Of Many Gifts." The New York Times (October 3, 2003). Accessed May 6, 2016. http://www.nytimes.com/2003/10/03/arts/art-review-el-greco-bearer-of-many-gifts.html?pagewanted=all.

13 Munroe, Myles, Passing It On: Growing Your Future Leaders (New York: Hachette Book Group, 2011), 24.

14 Quoted in: Noble, James Phillips, Words and Images that Seep into the Soul (Eugene, Oregon: Resource Publications, 2013), 155.

15 McKeown, Greg, Essentialism: The Disciplined Pursuit of Less (New York: Crown Business, 2014), 5.

16 Ibid., 10.

17 Maraboli, Steve, Life, the Truth, and Being Free (Port Washington, New York: A Better Today Publishing, 2014).

18 "Waking up early." Wikipedia. Accessed May 6, 2016. https://en.wikipedia.org/wiki/Waking_up_early.

19 Ibid.

20 Laino, Charlene. "Early Birds Get Better Grades." WebMD (June 9, 2008). Accessed April 23, 2016. http://www.webmd.com/sleep-disorders/news/20080609/early-birds-get-better-grades.

21 King, Stephen, Danse Macabre (New York: Gallery Books, 1981), 88.

22 Getty, J. Paul, How To Be Rich (New York: Jove Books, 1986).

23 King, Jr., Martin Luther, Strength to Love (Minneapolis: Fortress Press, 2010), 32.

24 "Infidelity Statistics," Menstuff. Accessed February 10, 2016. http://www.menstuff.org/issues/byissue/infidelitystats.html.

25 Ingall, Marjorie. "The Financial Secret That Could Ruin Your Relationship." SELF (May 17, 2012). Accessed December 28, 2015. http://www.self.com/wellness/relationships/2012/05/money-and-marriage/.

26 Mecia, Tony. "Poll: 13 million Americans commit financial infidelity." CreditCards.com (February 2, 2016). Accessed April 8, 2016. http://www.creditcards.com/credit-card-news/financial-infidelity-poll-secret-account.php. Accessed 8 April 2016.

27 Saltz, Gail, Anatomy of a Secret Life: The Psychology of Living a Lie (New York: Broadway Books, 2006).

Carey, Benedict. "The Secret Lives of Just About Everybody." The New York Times (January 11, 2005). Accessed February 3, 2016. http://www.nytimes.com/2005/01/11/health/psychology/the-secret-lives-of-just-about-everybody.html?_r=0.

Sherman, Beth. "Leading a Double Life Is More Common Than Many Suspect." Los Angeles Times (November 29, 1992). Accessed May 6, 2016. http://articles.latimes.com/1992-11-29/news/vw-2591_1_double-life.

28 "Directory of Mark Twain's maxims, quotations, and various opinions: TRUTH." www.twainquotes.com. Accessed December 20, 2015. http://www.twainquotes.com/Truth.html.

29 Ford-Martin, Paula. "Attitude and Behavior – Changing attitudes to change behavior, Changing behavior to influence attitudes." Psychology Encyclopedia. Accessed May 6, 2016. http://psychology.jrank.org/pages/52/Attitude-Behavior.html.

30 Huntsman, Jon M., Winners Never Cheat—Even in Difficult Times (Upper Saddle River, New Jersey: Pearson Education, 2011), 89-90.

31 Ibid., 91.

32 Quoted in: Durant, Will, The Story of Philosophy (New York: Simon & Schuster, 1961), 76.

33 Kerry Patterson, Joseph Grenny, David Maxfield, Ron McMillan, Al Switzler, Influencer: The Power to Change Anything (New York: McGraw-Hill, 2008), 4.

34 Little, Steven S., The Milkshake Moment: Overcoming Stupid Systems, Pointless Policies, and Muddled Management to Realize Real Growth (Hoboken, New Jersey: John Wiley & Sons, 2008), 3-7.

35 Mandela, Nelson, Long Walk to Freedom: The Autobiography of Nelson Mandela (New York: Little, Brown and Company, 1995), 391.

36 Fein, Esther B. "Book Notes." The New York Times (November 20, 1991). Accessed January 4, 2016. http://www.nytimes.com/1991/11/20/books/book-notes-059091.html.

37 Frankl, Victor E., Man's Search for Meaning (Boston: Beacon Press, 2006), 66.

38 Quoted in: Frankl, Victor E., Man's Search for Meaning (Boston: Beacon Press, 2006), 76.

39 Frankl, Victor E., Man's Search for Meaning (Boston: Beacon Press, 2006), 89.

40 Frankl, Victor E., Man's Search for Meaning (Boston: Beacon Press, 2006), 105.

41 Laurence Day. Used with permission.

42 McHale, Brandee. "Why are so many millennials unemployed?" CNBC (December 4, 2015). Accessed May 9, 2016. http://www.cnbc.com/2015/12/03/why-are-so-many-millennials-unemployed-commentary.html.

43 Jobs, Steve. "2005 Stanford Commencement Address," Stanford News (June 14, 2005,). Accessed May 6, 2016. https://news.stanford.edu/2005/06/14/jobs-061505/.

44 "Ford factory workers get 40-hour week," History. Accessed May 1, 2016. http://www.history.com/this-day-in-history/ford-factory-workers-get-40-hour-week.

45 Quoted in: Grant, George. "Unstring the Bow," Grantian Florilegium (June 15, 2012). Accessed May 6, 2016. http://grantian.blogspot. com/2012/06/unstring-bow.html.

46 Clason, George S., The Richest Man in Babylon (New York: Signet, 1988), 14.

47 Clason, George S., The Richest Man in Babylon (New York: Signet, 1988), 20.

48 King, Jr., Martin Luther. "'Remaining Awake Through a Great Revolution,' Address at Morehouse College Commencement, June 2, 1959," Martin Luther King, Jr. And The Global Freedom Struggle. Accessed February 22, 2016. http://kingencyclopedia.stanford.edu/ encyclopedia/documentsentry/remaining_awake_2_ june_1959.1.html#fn1.

49 Bennett, William J., The Book of Virtues: A Treasury of Great Moral Stories (New York: Simon & Schuster, 1993), 198-199.

50 Mandino, Og, The Greatest Salesman in the World (New York: Bantam Books, 1985).

51 Mandino, Og, The Greatest Salesman in the World, Part II: The End of the Story (New York: Bantam Books, 1989).

52 Rath, Tom, Vital Friends: The People You Can't Afford To Live Without (New York: Gallup Press, 2006).

53 Renvoisé, Patrick and Christophe Morin, Neuromarketing: Understanding the "Buy Buttons" in Your Customer's Brain (SalesBrain LLC, 2005).

54 Hsu, Jeremy. "The Secrets of Storytelling: Why We Love a Good Yarn," Scientific American (August 1, 2008). Accessed May 12, 2016. http:// www.scientificamerican.com/article/the-secrets-of-storytelling/.

55 Cardillo, ER, CE Watson, GL Schmidt, A Kranjec, and A Chatterjee. "From novel to familiar: tuning the brain for metaphors," Neuroimage 59.4 (February 2012): 3212-3221. Accessed June 10, 2016. http://www. ncbi.nlm.nih.gov/pubmed/22155328.

56 Guber, Peter, Tell to Win: Connect, Persuade, and Triumph with the Hidden Power of Story (New York: Crown Business, 2011).

57 "Directory of Mark Twain's maxims, quotations, and various opinions: SPEECH." www.twainquotes.com. Accessed May 6, 2016. http://www.twainquotes.com/Speech.html.

58 Smith, Paul, Lead With A Story: A Guide to Crafting Business Narratives That Captivate, Convince, and Inspire (New York: AMACOM, 2012).

59 Matthew Davis. Used with permission.

60 Strauss, Valerie. "Nelson Mandela on the power of education," The Washington Post (December 5, 2013). Accessed February 15, 2016. https://www.washingtonpost.com/news/answer-sheet/wp/2013/12/05/nelson-mandelas-famous-quote-on-education/.

61 "Give Said the Little Stream." Words by Fanny J. Crosby. Music by William B. Bradbury.

62 Quoted in: Bolz-Weber, Nadia, Salvation on the Small Screen? 24 Hours of Christian Television (New York: Seabury Books, 2008), 123.

63 Quoted in: Korrapati, Dr. Raghu, 108 Pearls of Wisdom for Every College Student (New Delhi, India: Diamond Pocket Books, 2011).

64 Elle Skeen. Used with permission.

65 Henley, William Ernest, "Invictus," The Oxford Book of English Verse: 1250-1900. Edited by Arthur Quiller-Couch (Oxford: Oxford University Press, 1919), 842.

ABOUT THE AUTHOR

Steven A. Hitz describes himself as a Baby Boomer with a Millennial heart. He studies, thinks like, celebrates, and advises what he calls "a great new generation." As a company founder, president, and CEO, he employed more than 10,000 Millennials. Plus he was a lay pastor of a congregation of 20- to 30-somethings.

Steve is a founding member of Launching Leaders Worldwide Inc., which offers the Launching Leaders book and online course, helping individuals examine their lives, determine where they are now, where they want to be, and how to create their future while embracing their faith.

He is an entrepreneur at heart, involved in varied businesses including insurance, banking, farming/cattle, and franchise operations. His business experience, coupled with advice from mentors and other forward thinkers (he is a voracious reader), helped him shape the principles contained in this book.

Steve has been honored with a Global Business & Interfaith Peace Medal from the Religious Freedom & Business Foundation, in collaboration with the United Nations Global Compact Business for Peace platform, the Global Compact Network Korea, and the United Nations Alliance of Civilizations (2018).

He is married to the amazing Ginger L. Hitz. They are blessed with three sons, two daughters, and ten beloved grandchildren and counting.

Contact Steve by visiting:
www.LLworldwide.org

Made in the USA
San Bernardino, CA
02 January 2020